To George.
'blessings'

Willie Bell

"Coach Bill Bell will always be fondly remembered and appreciated by everyone associated with Liberty University. He came on board at a time when my father was building Liberty — literally — from the ground up. Coach Bell's success as a professional soccer player and coach in the United Kingdom made him a role model for me and my fellow classmates at Liberty, but Coach Bell's love and concern for students and his testimony for Jesus Christ made the biggest impact on young lives. He molded every young man who played soccer for him into a true Champion for Christ."

— JERRY FALWELL JR.,
PRESIDENT OF LIBERTY UNIVERSITY

"Willie Bell was a tremendous player, coach and leader of young men. Above all, he was an outstanding individual who gave a great deal to the game of soccer. This book provides an insightful read into Willie's life and faith in and around the game."
— BRUCE ARENA, COACH, MLS LOS ANGELES GALAXY
USMNT WORLD CUP, 2002 & 2006

THE LIGHT
AT THE END
OF THE
TUNNEL

From the English Football Leagues
to English Prisons —
the Story of One Life
Dedicated to Making
a Difference

by WILLIAM BELL

with RON STARNER

The Light at the End of the Tunnel
by William Bell with Ron Starner

ISBN 13: 978-1-935986-93-5

First print edition, July 2014

Published by Liberty Mountain Publishing. Printed in the U.S.A.
Liberty Mountain Publishing
Lynchburg, VA
www.LibertyMountainPublishing.com

Cover design, illustrations, and typography by Bob Gravlee
Interior layout and design by Bob Gravlee

All quotations are from the King James Version

Contact the author – Ron Starner – at ron.starner@conway.com.

**A DIVISION OF
LIBERTY UNIVERSITY**

*This book is dedicated to my dear wife Mary,
faithful friend and mother, always encouraging —
a woman after God's own heart — and deeply loved.*

Contents

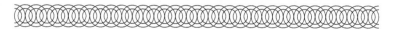

CONTENTS

FOREWORD

A generous person will prosper;
whoever refreshes others will be refreshed.
PROVERBS 11:25,
NEW INTERNATIONAL VERSION (NIV)

Coach and Mrs. Bell have lived this verse out since I first had the privilege and opportunity to meet them in the spring of 1987. I was investigating schools during my senior year and was primarily concerned with finding the right fit for me in terms of soccer. I had not heard about Liberty University or Coach Bell at the time, but my mom and dad decided to drive me up for a visit and see the campus. After spending five minutes with the Bell family I was sold on where I needed to be and why I needed to be there. Their willingness to embrace me and my family regardless of my abilities was quickly apparent and we felt refreshed by simply being around them. It was clear that if I came to Liberty that soccer would be my ministry and it would provide me a platform to share my faith with others. Coach Bell shined a light on what my abilities with a ball were intended to be about, and that included me sharing the Gospel with the people I came in contact with. I took a step of faith that weekend and committed to attend LU and become a part of the Liberty University soccer family and have not left the Mountain since that time.

I was blessed to have spent 4 years as a student-athlete with Coach and Mrs. Bell serving as a 2nd set of parents for me as I was away from my home in Atlanta, Georgia. During this time they provided guidance, direction, love and discipline to prepare and equip me for life after the ball stopped bouncing. In 1992, God opened up a door for me to start my apprenticeship as Coach Bell's assistant coach with the men's soccer program. It was an opportunity of a lifetime to learn the game of soccer from one of the top coaches in the country and put into practice what it meant to be generous and refresh others daily. Coach Bell was all about investing his life into the life of others and even though I thought spending time with him would provide me with the soccer knowledge and expertise from a strategy or tactics viewpoint (which he did), I was completely wrong about soccer being the primary focus. My daily time with him provided me with a blueprint for success as a coach, mentor, father, son, friend, leader. The lessons learned during my nine years as his assistant proved invaluable and help guide and direct how I live my life now as a father, coach, friend and mentor.

Personally, Coach Bell is an honest person who possesses a strong desire to succeed without compromising his Christian faith. He taught our group of men how to develop outstanding leadership qualities and become reliable and conscientious. His passion and commitment to uncompromised excellence allowed us to be successful on and off the field of play.

Professionally, Coach Bell is a man of character and integrity. He constantly reminded us to let our yes be yes and our no be no, and he lived this out for us daily. His willingness to serve others and lead by example imprinted the lives of each member that came through our program and allowed us to become better servants during our time under his leadership.

I will leave you with my favorite recruiting story from one day during a visit from a student-athlete. Coach Bell had asked the potential player to put together some film so we could evaluate him and consider him for a roster spot. The player responded "Would you like me to send you some film of me juggling the ball so you can see what I can do?" Coach Bell leaned forward in his chair, focused, intense, and replied "Aye son, the people in the circus can juggle, but they cann-e (can't) play soccer." In the midst of me holding back tears as I fought from laughing out loud, I looked at the recruit and told him game film would be fine. — *Jeff Alder, Head Men's Soccer Coach, Liberty University*

PREFACE

It is always an exciting moment when the players enter the tunnel right before a soccer match. An almost eerie quiet settles over everyone. Few words are exchanged. The hustle and bustle of the dressing room — with all the last-minute instructions being given by the coaches, the jocular banter among the players, and the uniforms being donned — has given way to a moment of serious focus.

It was a time of quiet reflection for me. I would retreat into my own thoughts and plans for the player I would be facing that day. I would then offer up a short prayer for protection.

The clickety-click of soccer boots on the concrete was like music to my ears. I was exactly where I wanted to be — entering the great arena where the skills I had honed for years would be used, and where the chants of the fans would echo around the stadium.

This was all part of my 21 years in the English Football League. Gradually, I allowed myself to become so programmed to the game that I became obsessed with it. My mind constantly dwelt on football. I thought of nothing else. My life was controlled by a sport demanding my all.

We all travel through a tunnel of sorts, continually aiming for something intangible — perfection. I was searching for a better life. I played in exotic places, met many famous people, played for the most successful team of that era in Britain, but never found the elusive happiness I so desperately sought.

Not until I was 40 years of age did I find the peace and happiness I was so hungry to capture. That's when I discovered what that light at the end of the tunnel really was. — *William Bell*

INTRODUCTION

On a sweltering July 1981 day in a small office on the campus of Liberty Baptist College in Lynchburg, Va., I met the man I would know as "Coach Bell" for the next 30 years of my life.

The first thing I noticed about him was that he was stout and resolute. Harboring a quiet confidence honed over decades of accomplishment on the hallowed fields of Scottish and English soccer, William Bell was entering his third season as the men's soccer coach at this small Baptist college in south central Virginia.

How did a living British sports legend end up coaching kids at a small Christian school in Appalachia? How did a man who lined up against Pelé, George Best and Peter Shilton in the highest professional tier accept the challenge to mold young men who were amateurs in the sport of soccer?

The answer to that question is the purpose of this book. Just as any life is more than the sum of its parts, the story of Bell's life is more than a collection of starting lineups, substitution decisions, player transfers, college recruits and missions to Africa and Great Britain.

The Light at the End of the Tunnel is, at its essence, a story of life, loss and redemption, with a call to action that only a life forged through adversity could teach. The reader will see this truth woven through every chapter, every episode, of Bell's life.

That Bell would ask me, one of his former college players, to help him write his book is one of the most humbling honors of my life. Bell's story is transcendent and worthy of attention. The accounts shared in this work are totally his. I have served merely as the scribe and editor whose job is to tie these various stories together and help the subject extract his life's principle themes.

I have enjoyed every minute of it, and not just because Bell has lived a rich and rewarding life. My joy has come in getting to know the man all over again, 26 years after I last suited up for his Liberty Flames.

To know Bell is to appreciate his warmth, humility and genuine love for people. He has always supremely loved his family, including his wife, Mary, and three children, William Jr., Andrew and Caroline.

But what sets Bell apart from most men is his unparalleled ability to love his players, fellow coaches, opponents, and everyone else he meets. One of the toughest competitors ever produced on the fields of Scottish soccer, Bell grew up to become a man whose heart was even greater than his legend.

Whether it's helping impoverished players find their way from Africa to the United States, or ministering to the needs of young men imprisoned in England, Bell has devoted his life to caring for the hearts of the hurting.

From 1982 to 1986, I witnessed these qualities on display every day as I grew under his coaching at Liberty. But the real payoff for me came in the years that followed, as his example of character and integrity impacted every area of my life.

It is a true privilege to help Bell share these lessons with the readers of this book. *The Light at the End of the Tunnel* packs more punch, twists and turns than a World Cup final that ends on a golden goal.

That's true because Bell never compromised in his life. Therefore, it's only fitting that his autobiography not compromise either.

Once you know Bell, you will understand how the coach would never have it any other way. — *Ron Starner*

THE MISGUIDED PURSUIT

William Bell came of age during an era in which soccer was not just the prime sports passion of his Scottish and English brethren; it was, for many of them, their entire life.

Die-hard fans of British soccer have long had a history of cheering fanatically for their favorite teams and players, while also disparaging — often unmercifully — the teams and players they despised.

Too often, this passion has boiled over into tragedy, such as the 1989 Hillsborough Stadium disaster when 96 fans were crushed to death in Sheffield, England, during the FA Cup semifinal between Liverpool and Nottingham Forest. Eight years prior, 38 fans were injured during the FA Cup final between Wolverhampton and Tottenham.

Liverpool fans have become synonymous with tragedy. In the past, many of them would use the 1958 Munich air disaster involving Manchester United to mock their opponents.

On Feb. 6, 1958, seven players on United died as their plane skidded off the snow-covered runway in Munich. An eighth player would die two weeks later from injuries he sustained in the fiery crash. Bobby Charlton, one of the greatest legends in British soccer history, survived that crash.

For decades, some Liverpool fans would taunt United with chants of "Munich," making reference to that black day.

This is the stuff of which British soccer is made — forged in the fires of passion so intense that it often blinds the sensibilities of otherwise sensible people.

Bell himself is no stranger to this passion. Reminiscing about his own career as a player and coach at the highest levels of European professional soccer, he admits that he too was often blinded by this crazed belief in his own team's superiority.

It is this very life-and-death attitude toward their sport that elicits such intense reactions from fans, players, coaches, officials, the media and others involved in the pastime of promoting soccer in the British Isles.

In London, Manchester, Liverpool, Birmingham, Glasgow, Dublin, Cork, Belfast, and many places in between, nothing evokes stronger emotions than rooting for one's chosen soccer team and pulling against all opponents.

While tragic incidents such as the one in Sheffield in 1989 have largely been avoided in recent years, the same raw emotions often still lurk just barely beneath the surface.

But back in the days when Bell played and coached in England and played in Scotland — the 1960s and 1970s — there was very little to keep such emotions in check.

It is this foundation — where supporters of teams brought both the greatest love and the most intense hatred to the pitch for each and every game — that underpinned Bell's professional career.

It would be later in life that he would learn that so much of this intensity was a misguided pursuit. — *Ron Starner*

The Light at the End of the Tunnel

"For whosoever shall call upon the name of the Lord shall be saved."

— ROMANS 10:13

My wife's prayer was answered.

One evening, after losing a game as head coach of Birmingham City in the English Premier League, I came home to my family. As usual, they had the good sense to avoid me. Winning games at the highest level of professional soccer was not only the driving passion of my life in my 20s and 30s; it was my world.

Little did I know that my whole world was about to change on September 5, 1977.

As soon as I entered our house in England, my wife went into a separate room to pray. Her prayer was simple: "Dear God, please help my family."

The next morning, the chairman of the Birmingham City Football Club called me in to his office to tell me that I was fired.

Having become one of the many casualties of the game that I had devoted my entire life to, I very soon came to the realization that I had been a fool. I had sacrificed my family for the game of soccer. For the first time in years, I had time to review my life and where it had taken me.

When I was a young man, I had the opportunity to represent

my country, Scotland, as one of the top eleven soccer players in the nation. As I walked on to the turf of Hampden Park in Glasgow to face Pele and Brazil, I remember thinking, "This is the ultimate. I have reached the pinnacle of my life."

Soccer was everything to me. Ever since I was a small child, I had dreamed of playing for professional clubs. Every evening, my dad would have to come looking for me, as I would be outside somewhere kicking a soccer ball under the street lights after dark. I idolized the members of my local soccer team, St. Mirren. Sports drove me. I excelled at swimming and enjoyed cricket, but my passion was soccer.

As the years passed and my skills progressed, I was chosen to play for a junior team in our hometown area of Scotland. I still longed to make it to the "big time." I worked hard to improve my craft. Training sessions, as well as the games, were opportunities for me to do the best I could to get better.

One day, a Scottish Second Division side named Queens Park offered me the opportunity to play for their team. Needless to say, I accepted. During this time, I was studying and working as an engineer at a local factory, even as I continued to dream of making it all the way to the top of the professional soccer ranks one day.

That chance arrived. Leeds United, one of the most storied clubs in all of British soccer, invited me to join their squad. By this time, I was married, so Mary and I accepted the offer and moved across the border to England.

During my time with Leeds United, I was able to travel around the world to compete in soccer matches. Back home, I was hailed as a hero. My goal had been reached.

Yet there was still a void in my life. An emptiness in the pit of my soul that the cheering crowds and adoring fans could not fill. Even my wife and three beautiful children could not fill this emptiness inside of me.

After a lengthy and successful career at Leeds, Leicester City, and Brighton & Hove Albion, I retired from playing to become head coach of Birmingham City, another large professional club in England. They were more than generous toward me and my family. They paid me a good salary, and every two years they would present me with the keys to a brand new Mercedes-Benz.

On the outside, it would have appeared that all was well in the Bell household. But this was not the case. My passion for the game consumed me to the exclusion of my family. Results on the field began to dictate my mood at home. My wife and children often felt the backlash of fury after I would lose a crucial game. In essence, soccer had become my god.

Yes, I had attained my boyhood dream and more. I had received a medal from Her Majesty the Queen of England and had tea with presidents. I had experienced the adulation of thousands — but I had failed the ones who loved me the most, the same people whom I loved the most.

I attended church every Sunday, but I hadn't been listening or paying attention to the service. There, sitting in the pew, I would be plotting team strategy.

After my dismissal from Birmingham as team manager, I now had the time to listen to those I had ignored for so long. When my firing was announced on television that evening, many friends called to console me.

One dear friend invited my wife Mary and me out to dinner. Upon accepting that invitation, little did I know that at long last I was about to fill the void in my life and learn the true meaning of peace and happiness.

That evening at dinner my friend Norman Gidney asked me to go on a short visit to the United States to take some time to contemplate my future. He and his wife Carol kindly offered to care for our three children while we were gone.

Norman wanted us to visit a friend of his in Ohio for a few days. We were soon on our way to the small town of Massillon, Ohio — a place that would change my life forever.

A charming couple by the name of Harry and Shirley Hudson warmly welcomed us upon our arrival in Massillon.

They had even donned a plaid hat and cape in honor of our Scottish heritage.

We arrived emotionally bruised and battered from the events of the past few days. The press had been hounding us in an attempt to publish more news about my firing. Against that backdrop, it was such a relief to sit down with folks who did not want to discuss soccer or anything pertaining to my former job.

We immediately sensed a peace in the home of this dear couple. Norman and Carol, our friends back in England, had not told us that their friend in Ohio was the pastor of a church.

The following Sunday, we went to church as usual, only this time there wasn't anything usual about church. Upon entering the little sanctuary in Massillon, I sensed a distinct difference in the people. I could not put my finger on it, but immediately I knew that the people had something I did not.

It was the love of Christ. They had a personal relationship with Jesus and they worshipped Him as their Lord and Savior.

As the service drew to a close, I found myself asking God to let me be like these people. I knew in my heart that Jesus was real and that He had died on Calvary for my sins — and what was more, He had risen again and granted me eternal life. All I had to do was receive Him as my personal Savior.

As I felt the tears well up, I also felt a great release as my cares and worries were swept away. I was His and He was mine. It was all so simple and yet so powerful.

We left Calvary Chapel, the place of our new birth, with a new song in our hearts.

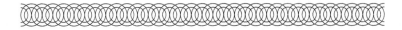

Scottish Dreams:
Life and Loss

*"Train up a child in the way he should go,
and when he is old he will not depart from it."*
— PROVERBS 22:6

Growing up in Scotland during the 1940s and 1950s, I wasn't always singing. In fact, I would learn a lot of life lessons that would shape me dramatically in my formative years.

I was born in the working-class town of Johnstone, Renfrewshire, on Sept. 3, 1937, and like most kids of that era, I couldn't find enough daylight to cram in all the activity that I craved each and every day.

Spending evenings on the streets of Scotland while playing under the lights was the norm for Scottish children. I was no exception. Every night, my friends and I could be found kicking a soccer ball on the street where I lived. My Mom worked at the local mill most nights. This left Dad in charge of my brother Dennis and I.

In winter, the darkness would settle in early. When I was just 8 years old, I remember Dad warning me to be home before dark or I would face the consequences. I never dreamed that Dad would actually punish me.

Darkness came, but my friends and I wanted to finish our small-sided game of soccer. When I finally came home, feeling on top of the world because we had won our game, I was greeted by a very angry father. He had spent the last hour worrying about me.

"Where have you been?" he asked.

"Playing football," I said.

"OK, over the bed," Dad said as he undid his belt.

Yes, Dad gave me a beating, and yes, it hurt. No, I did not stay out late again.

I had loving parents who cared enough to discipline. Did I like it at the time? No. Did it work? Yes. Do I wish that more kids had parents who loved them enough to correct them when they make bad choices? Yes.

It would be many years later when I would fully learn the true value of a loving father, mother and brother Dennis.

When I was 10, our family would spend our Saturdays traveling by train to Greenock to visit my grandparents. I enjoyed these outings immensely. A big reason for this was my namesake Uncle Willie, who lived with my grandparents. I loved and adored my Uncle Willie.

Unfortunately, Willie had suffered from pneumatic fever as a child. The illness had left him with a weak heart. He found it difficult to breathe. Many days, he would sit on the edge of his bed gasping for breath. He received weekly injections to help him survive, but I always sensed a deep sadness in my parents that let me know that something was seriously wrong with Uncle Willie.

The family would joke and try to keep everyone's spirits up, but I remained very much aware that Uncle Willie's life was drawing to a close. I can still picture the small living room where our family gathered while Willie's life came to an end.

Although Granny was a devout Catholic who constantly prayed for each of us by name, Willie was not a believer. It was a heartbreaking situation — a good man dying with no hope. And none of us were equipped to share the love of God with him.

Two weeks after that, gathering on a wet and dreary day on a hillside in Greenock, I attended my first funeral. My precious Uncle Willie was gone.

Before we left for the cemetery, a Catholic priest came to the house at the request of my grandmother. He lingered for a few minutes, but aware of Willie's rejection of the church, the priest left.

The memory of that bleak day is imprinted indelibly on my mind. I stood with my grandfather, my Dad and his two brothers. The rain was falling on the leaves of the trees with a gentle pitter patter as the grave lay open. No words of encouragement were said. Our hearts were one in enveloping sadness.

I heard my father say to my Uncle Johnny, "Don't you think we should say something?"

Uncle Johnny said the Lord's Prayer, but still I was left with a hollowness in my being. There was no peace in our hearts.

The family turned away to walk down the hill, uncertain of Willie's eternal home. To this day, I miss my jovial Uncle Willie. I even became an engineer just like him, because I loved him so much.

But I also knew that I never wanted to feel as hollow ever again.

That wasn't the only important lesson that I would learn as a child. At age 12, I was living in Paisley, Scotland, and attending the East School. The local School Swimming Gala was about to take place.

I had been training hard for the 100-yard freestyle race, an event in which I would have the opportunity to become the West of Scotland Junior Champion. My swim coach told me that my nearest rival was a full second behind me in his time. If I could win, I knew I would become the school's hero.

On the evening of the gala, I won two prizes, one of which was the coveted trophy for the West of Scotland Championship. I was beaming with pride the next day as our school headmaster sent me around the classrooms to display the silver trophy.

A few months later, the grand finale of the swim season was

set to take place with the champions of all age levels competing for the title of Scottish National Champion. I was the youngest competitor, so therefore I was allowed an 18-second head start.

"Wow," I thought. "This should be easy."

Even though I was competing against grown men, I thought the handicap would be a great advantage for me.

I stood at the start, a 13-year-old boy alongside men. The starter's pistol cracked against the screams and cheers of the crowd. I was off.

Giving all that I could muster, I swam with gusto. When my fingers eventually touched the side of the pool, I quickly looked around to see where I had placed. Where had I finished?

It did not take me long to see that all of the other swimmers were resting with their elbows on the side of the pool. I had finished dead last.

I felt defeated and humiliated. Realizing that I had been completely outclassed, I went home deflated and demoralized.

I began to worry about returning to school on Monday. What would the other students think of me now? That day nobody mentioned the gala. In fact, no one had seemed even to know that I had been competing in the event.

I was relieved. Defeat was not something that I was used to. But the experience also taught me a great lesson in humility. I have never forgotten it since.

Many years later, when I would play for Leeds United in the top English Football League, I never took any of our opponents for granted, regardless of their record on the field.

It does not do us any harm to eat humble pie sometimes. It certainly was good for me.

My family would always vacation in Weymouth in the South of England. My favorite Aunt Madge and Uncle Ron lived there, and each year they would graciously open their home to us.

Aunt Madge was a marvelous cook and full of fun. And I greatly enjoyed being able to go fishing with my Uncle Ron off the Chesil Beach. One year, when I asked my Mom and Dad to allow me to stay with my relatives, my parents granted my wish.

Eventually, the anticipated short stay became three years of living with my aunt and uncle and their son, my young cousin Ronnie. I attended the local school where I was chosen to play on the Westham School soccer team. The physical education teacher there seemed to think that the fact I was Scottish meant I could play well.

As I walked home to Aunt Madge's house that day, I realized I would need a pair of football boots. I had left mine back home in Scotland.

Upon arriving home, I searched the house for a pair of cleats. I was delighted to find Uncle Ron's old soccer shoes in the bottom of a cupboard. I tried them on, only to discover that they were two sizes too big for my feet.

"Never mind," I thought. "I will put on three extra pairs of socks."

By the evening prior to the game, a pair of shining soccer shoes sporting new white laces were lying at the foot of my bed. I had polished them until they looked fairly new. It was a labor of love.

The day of the game dawned. A crowd of six spectators attended my big day. We were playing against our school's biggest rival, Portland. As the match drew to a close, our team was happy to be holding our opponent to a scoreless draw.

Then it happened. We were granted a penalty kick. All eyes flew to our P.E. teacher, who yelled out, "Give it to Bell, the Scottish lad! Let him take it!"

As I approached the penalty spot, exactly 12 yards from the goal, the whole world seemed to stand still. I approached the ball with my head bent, knowing exactly where I wanted to aim it.

I kicked the ball, and just as I did my oversized boot caught in the grass, making the ball travel in the direction opposite to where I had intended. I felt humiliated.

But then something very unusual happened. As the ball

traveled slowly toward the goal, the goalkeeper dove in the direction of where I had intended to shoot the ball. I couldn't believe it when the soccer ball slowly trickled into the net.

The six fans, my entire team and I were jubilant. A perfectly taken penalty shot, everyone thought. But I knew better.

All I could think of was my determination to buy a new pair of soccer boots as soon as I could save up enough money from my paper route. I accepted the adulation that day, but I never tried to play in soccer cleats two sizes too big ever again.

Years later, upon my leaving the Westham School, the principal, Mr. Strathue, related to the student body the story of "the best penalty kick in the history of the school." To this day, Mr. Strathue has no idea that it was actually the worst penalty kick ever taken to land in the back of the net.

For about the next two and a half years, I was very happy living with my Aunt Madge, Uncle Ron and cousin Ronnie in Weymouth. My days there were filled with carefree abandonment. I fished, played soccer, and enjoyed being a member of the school cricket team. I also enjoyed swimming, of course.

My favorite pastime, however, was beachcombing after a storm. My uncle allowed me to use his row boat to row across the short stretch of water from the mainland to Chesil Beach, which stretched for miles on the ocean. My cousin Ronnie and I would rush to the beach as soon as a storm ended, our hearts racing in anticipation of the expected treasures we would find swept to shore by the huge waves from the sea.

We would find all sorts of valuable items that had fallen overboard from ships tossed at sea. The treasures could be large planks of perfectly good timber, or brass and copper items that could fetch good prices on the market. My most memorable discovery was a solid brass porthole from a ship. I had been walking along the shore one day when I spotted a piece of brass sticking up among the pebbles. As I bent toward the sand to retrieve it, my heart raced with excitement. An intact porthole emerged.

Delirious with glee, I staggered home with my newfound treasure. I was jubilant, as I knew that brass sold by the pound and this treasure seemed to weigh a ton. I would always keep a glass jar to contain the proceeds from the sale of my booty.

When I would accompany my Uncle Ron on his fishing trips, he always made sure that I was paid my fair share for the haul. We fished in longboats with a crew of eight or so, heady stuff for a boy of just 15. The shoals of fish — known as a stray of mackerel — could be seen from the shore. The crew would sit on the beach looking out to sea until one of the fishermen would shout, "They are straying!"

Immediately, all hands rushed to push the longboat into the sea. The net was dropped to surround the fish, and when full, two men on shore would begin to pull the net inland. Four other men would jump off the boat to help in landing the catch. I would always remain in the boat until the fish were safely ashore.

The catch would be transferred into large baskets, which were then transported to the mainland to the waiting fish merchant. As I proudly strode back home with my share of 12 mackerel on a string and the prospect of a payout, I never dreamed of the tragic circumstances that would come on the very shores that had produced my great joy.

The day arrived when it was time for me to return home to Paisley, Scotland. My parents felt that I would have better opportunities for a job in Scotland. It is impossible to explain the heaviness in my heart as I said my farewells to the family that had showered me with so much love and acceptance — Aunt Madge, Uncle Ron and cousin Ronnie. They would forever hold a special place in my heart. I boarded the train back home to Scotland with a deep sadness. I was returning home to an industrial city, a far cry from my beloved seaside home in Weymouth.

On arriving at the Paisley station, I glanced around hopefully, but there was no one there to greet me. So I began my walk home. Upon reaching home, my first greeting to my mother were these words: "What a dump of a town." Later, I regretted those remarks.

The rain poured down, adding to the dreariness of the day. Upon retiring to bed that night, my mind drifted back to Weymouth, the sea, and the dear family I had left behind. I had never felt so sorrowful in my young life. But it was time to begin another chapter.

Eventually, I became an apprentice engineer with Albion Motor Works in Scotstoun Glasgow. Early one Monday morning, I was on my way to work when I saw Uncle Johnny, my father's oldest brother, coming toward me. I immediately sensed an emergency.

"Is your Dad at home, Billy?" he inquired.

"Yes," I replied. "Is there something wrong?"

Uncle Johnny told me that my beloved Uncle Ron and his son Ronnie were missing and presumed drowned.

I was devastated. It had only been a few short years since I had left Weymouth. I spent my annual holidays there and had remained very close to my family there.

My mind was in turmoil. I immediately thought of Aunt Madge. I knew she must be in agony. I just wanted to comfort her at that moment.

The outcome was slowly revealed. The bodies of both Uncle Ron and his son Ronnie were recovered by the coast guard in four feet of water. The accident had happened when the crew members were out fishing on Remembrance Sunday. It was a bitterly cold day. On the return trip, the flat-bottomed boat capsized into the fast-flowing water called Littlesea. The crew and young Ronnie made it to shore, but their hands were too cold to undo the ropes of the small crafts along the shore. Ronnie, then just 14 years old, saw his father, who could not swim, holding onto the boat, and decided to return to help him. Ronnie sacrificed his life in an attempt to save his father. The last the crew saw of them was both hanging on to the upturned boat before being swept away.

I can never fully explain the devastation I felt that day. Two of my beloved family had been snatched away in such a terrible fashion. My young cousin had shown tremendous bravery. In the Bible, John 15:13 states that "Greater love hath no man than this, that a man lay down his life for his friends."

My cousin had indeed earned the title of "man." I also became a man that day as I faced up to the harsh realities of life. Though I still miss them dearly, I will always treasure my memories of the two dear souls who had impacted my life in such a profound way, defining the true meaning of love for me.

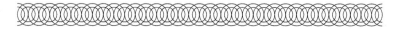

The Dream Fulfilled: The Call from Leeds United

*"Trust in the Lord with all thine heart, and lean not
on thine own understanding. In all thy ways acknowledge Him, and
He shall direct thy paths."*
— PROVERBS 3:5-6

While tragedy brought ample heartache to my family during
my formative years, soccer brought me joy.

Junior football was a very happy time for me. I never felt
like I was under pressure, as my performances on the pitch
seemed to satisfy virtually everyone who watched me play.
Many professional team scouts would regularly attend my junior
football games in search of talented players.

One day, a scout from the Stoke City Football Club
approached me. He invited me to come to England and take a
look at the English First Division setup.

My father and I traveled to Stoke together on the train. I felt
very relaxed as I prepared myself to play in the try-out match.
My Dad sat in the stands with the team manager, Mr. Frank
Taylor. Dad enjoyed every minute of being the guest of such a
famous club.

When the match was over, I was invited to join the club.
Rather than immediately accept the job I had always dreamed of,
I asked the club if it would be possible to have a few days before I
made my decision. They agreed.

As we left the football grounds, I told my father that I did not like the big city. Stoke is an industrial city that's famous for its potteries where all the best English china is made.

Even though the lure to turn professional was great, I decided to inform Stoke City that I would continue to live in Paisley and fulfill my term as an apprentice engineer. I made the decision to keep playing as an amateur until the right professional club came calling — hopefully — with an offer.

The thrilling part of my visit to England was being invited to Maine Road to watch Manchester United play Anderlecht in the European Cup. Since Old Trafford, the hallowed home turf of United, did not have lights, the match was played at Maine Road.

So one night I watched the famed "Busby Babes" — eight of whom would die later in the horrible Munich plane crash of February 6, 1958 play a magnificent game. United won by seven goals. As I sat there and watched, I was mesmerized by the skills of such a storied team and clung to my dream to one day become a football star.

Upon my return to my native Scotland, I was invited to join the Neilston Juniors, a team that competed in the Ayrshire League. Club official Hammie Frew persuaded me to sign with the club. Even though I was offered a fee to sign as a professional, I chose to remain an amateur. I did this so that I would be free to sign for a professional team that I knew would come one day.

Playing for Neilston made me quite happy. Hammie proved to be a true friend. He always looked out for my best interests. I continued to enjoy playing and improving my skills. I made several good friends on the team. Life for me at this time was good.

Not long after this, a representative of Queens Park, the famous amateur team in the second division, approached me. David Leatham had been a player for this wonderful team, whose home stadium of Hampden Park hosted many international matches.

Leatham explained that Queens Park was very interested in signing me to play for them. To be able to play for this prestigious team at Scotland's national stadium would be a dream come true for me.

When my amateur status was confirmed, I joined the Queens Park club. To be able to continue working as an engineer and play against the top teams in Scotland gave me a great sense of pride and accomplishment.

Eventually, I was chosen to play for amateur Scotland. I learned of my selection to the national team while I was on the Renfrew Ferry coming home from work one evening.

A friend called me to say, "Congratulations, Willie, on being chosen to play for Scotland."

I muttered my gratitude while in a state of disbelief. I had come to know of this big step in my career only because my friend had read this news in the local paper.

My schedule was hectic, to say the least. I would rush home from working the nightshift each Saturday, change clothes quickly, and then rush to catch the bus to Hampden, where I would then board the team bus that would take us to the venue of our match.

I played against giants such as the Glasgow Rangers. I continued, however, wanting to become a professional soccer player. I just kept waiting for the right club to approach me with an offer.

Impatient with this waiting game, I decided to visit my local team, St. Mirren, and ask them if they might be interested in hiring me as a player. When I approached the team manager, Willie Reid, at his office, I did so with fear and trembling.

I knocked on his door, only to be greeted with a very terse and gruff, "Come in."

I stood in front of this man to plead my case. He looked me up and down and then asked who I played for.

The next thing I knew, he delivered the heartbreaking decision: "Naw," he said.

Just like that, my hopes were dashed with a single word.

I often wondered if Willie Reid ever thought of that day when a young lad stood in his office, only to be completely dismissed so readily.

This same young man would go on one day to play for his country at the highest level and become the regular starting fullback for the most exciting team in Great Britain, Leeds United, during their glory years.

My big break came when a colleague of mine at Albion Motors came to me and asked if I would like to turn professional and play for Leeds United. I was stunned. My heart raced as I realized my lifelong dream was about to come true.

I turned to my workmate and said, simply, "Yes, I am interested." I was ready to grasp the opportunity offered. "I will show the world what I am made of," I thought. "Just give me a chance."

I immediately requested the chance to call the secretary of Queens Park, as I did not want the committee managing the club to learn of my decision from the newspapers. I felt sad to be departing from such dear friends and very thankful for the time I had spent with a group of such honorable gentlemen.

Years later, I would return to Hampden Park to represent Scotland against Brazil. The committee and the players greeted me in the warmest way possible. I was overcome by their graciousness. They made me feel like they genuinely rejoiced with me in my career success.

Giddy with the best news of my life, I traveled to Leeds and signed the elusive professional forms.

FOUR

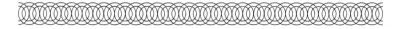

The Quest Begins

"Pride goeth before destruction,
and a haughty spirit before a fall."
— PROVERBS 16:18

I reported to Elland Road for the start of my first full season of training at Leeds United under the leadership of Don Revie. I was in great spirits even though I knew that pre-season training would be very demanding.

We had been told to go to bed early each evening in preparation for the grueling training that was to come. As that first great day dawned, I sailed through the warm-up period which took about 30 minutes.

That's when I noticed the telegraph poles laid out along each end of the field. "They must be laying some new telephone poles," I thought. Following our workout, we learned why the poles were there.

Relay teams consisting of six men each were formed. We were then instructed to carry a pole between us to the opposite end of the field, drop it, run back, touch the wall, and then return and carry the pole back to where we had started.

I could not believe that we were being asked to perform such a physically demanding and exhausting feat. Of course, the coaches knew that if one player did not pull his weight, the whole team would struggle. We all did as instructed.

After each practice, I would come home exhausted and fall into bed every evening, saying to Mary, "I don't know if I am going to make it."

One day, we were told that we would be going to the golf course. "Great!" I thought. We were about to be rewarded for all of our hard work with a relaxing game of golf.

My brief joy quickly disappeared when we were told to run the length of two fairways to exchange a baton with another team member, who would then do the same. I distinctly remember my team leading the relay race as my teammate Eddie Gray ran the final fairway in first place. We were overjoyed until Eddie collapsed before finishing the race.

Upon reflection, I actually admire Don Revie's coaching strategy. He knew that by forming teams we would all push each other to our limits. No one on the team ever wanted to let a fellow teammate down. As a result, each of us would dig down deep within ourselves to pull out the very last grain of effort.

Our first game of my first season at Leeds was against Sunderland, our arch rivals. Within minutes of the opening whistle, we all became aware of the indisputable fact that Sunderland could not compete with the fitness level of the Leeds players. It was a wonderful thing to know, beyond a shadow of a doubt, that we were the fittest team in the entire English First Division. This knowledge instilled great confidence in our team.

Looking back on those days, I now realize that we were on the threshold of an epic period that became known as the Revie Era.

We became known as the Revie Machine.

The season I joined Leeds, the club signed a tenacious little midfielder from Scotland named Eric Smith. Smith's main job was to win the ball back from the other team. Our manager, Jack Taylor would use him to stop the opponent's best players in the midfield area.

One of Smith's first games saw him matched against the very talented Welsh international Graham Moore. Before the game, Jack Taylor, gave clear instructions: "Smith must tackle Moore hard at all times and stop him from creating openings for his team." Everyone knew exactly what the coach meant.

Three minutes into the first half, Smith's two-footed tackle on Moore could be heard all over the stadium. The crack of breaking bone echoed through the arena. Both players remained down on the pitch.

I thought that Smith was trying to feign injury and fool the officials. I knew that if he got up, he would be issued a red card and ordered off the field. That's when the referee signaled for both teams' trainers to come onto the field.

Within minutes, the Leeds trainer, Les Cocker, was calling for a stretcher. It soon became apparent that Smith had badly broken his leg.

Moore rose to his feet and continued to play in the game. Smith finished the day in the hospital. His reward was a broken leg, along with his name entered into the official's handbook.

When I was a young lad, my father would boast about the exploits of Stanley Mathews. According to Dad, he was the most talented player ever born. We would often discuss Mathews, but my father and I would disagree.

When my father would heap praise on Mathews, I would say, "Come on, Dad. The game in your day was much slower and was played by part-time players." Still, I could never persuade my parents that the players of my day were faster and more skillful.

Years later, during my first season with Leeds United, we were scheduled to play Mathews' team, Stoke City, at Victoria Ground in Stoke. We enjoyed our pre-game team meal at the Station Hotel, located just 400 yards from the stadium. Following the meal, the team decided to go for a walk.

As we were strolling down the street, the team manager suddenly yelled out, "See that man over there, Willie? He is your opponent today."

I looked and saw a slender man with his hands in his pockets. He wore a trilby hat and was walking toward the stadium. He looked older than my father and was wizened beyond his years. This was my Dad's hero, Stanley Mathews, and I was scheduled to play against him.

I was suddenly looking at the man I had mocked for so long, and now I was being given the opportunity to prove my point. As I remembered the many arguments with my father over Mathews, I knew in my heart that this was a golden opportunity — one I had never dreamed would ever take place.

The game began with me thinking, "When Stan has the ball, I will play him inside." I knew that he always liked to run his opponent up the line.

As the play progressed, Stan would wait until I closed in on him and then pass the ball to a teammate. By 40 minutes into the game I was feeling very proud of myself.

Suddenly, the ball came to Stan's feet 30 yards from the Leeds penalty area. It was at this point that I found myself chasing a 50-year-old who displayed an incredible burst of speed over 5 yards — a speed that I could not even dream of matching.

He dragged the ball with his famous Mathews shuffle, and then boom! With the outside of his foot, Stan pushed the ball past me while he leaned inside — and then he was gone.

Reeling from shock, I attempted feebly to make up ground. It was a lost cause. Lunging at his heels, I managed to make contact, just enough to unbalance Stan, leading to a free kick for Stoke.

That was the only time that day that Mathews attempted to pass me. It was also a good lesson for me about my father's hero. Never again would I mock this legend.

Later in life, Mathews was knighted by the Queen of England in honor of his service on and off the field of play.

I now tell my children and grandchildren that I had the utmost privilege and honor of competing against a true legend of the game — Sir Stanley Mathews.

During the summer of 1966, the Scottish national team hosted Brazil in Glasgow. I was fortunate to be selected to suit up for Scotland as a defender. The highly talented Brazilians were preparing for the World Cup with the hope of retaining the most coveted trophy in all of football — the Jules Rimet Trophy.

Our Scottish team had spent long hours training at Largs, a seaside town, in preparation for this memorable event. Our national pride was at stake, and we were both mentally and physically ready to do our duty for our country.

We were very much aware that Brazil was the heavy favorite to win the World Cup.

During our pre-game chat in the locker room, my colleague Billy Bremner was instructed, "Billy, the first chance you get, let Pelé know that you mean business. He is the key to their success." Bremner gave the thumbs-up sign in response.

I believed that Pelé was one of the greatest soccer players in history. The next two hours would allow me to learn just how great he truly was.

The first half was swift and exciting, with both teams striving to open the scoring. True to form, Bremner stuck with Pelé, but was unable to hinder him in any way from receiving and distributing the ball. As halftime approached, Pelé came to receive a ball from his teammate in midfield. I watched in horror as Bremner took off, taking Pelé down from behind with a brutal tackle.

I felt sick and ashamed. As Pelé remained on the ground, the referee stopped the game to caution Bremner, saying, "If this were not an international game, you would be ordered off." I couldn't understand the referee's decision, as Billy certainly deserved a red card.

I ran across the field to determine the extent of Pelé's injury. As Pele looked around, I expected him to be angry with Bremner. Instead, he called his own teammate over and proceeded to tell him, "This was your fault. If you had given me a better ball, he would not have caught me." The teammate quickly rendered an apology.

I was amazed. The best player in the world addressed his

teammate rather than lash out at his opponent or the official for the hard foul.

The match ended in a 2-2 tie. The result would have been sweeter for me if my teammate had not resorted to unfair play.

On the other hand, I witnessed a true sportsman in action.

Today, when I hear the adulation that is given to Pelé, I know that he deserves it. He was not only the best soccer player in the world; he is also a splendid ambassador for the game, and for his country.

Leeds United was in the running for the league championship. Emotions were running high as the match against our great rivals Sunderland drew near. Sunderland was the only team that could catch us, with our team holding a slender one-point lead in the standings.

Horseplay was commonplace in the clubhouse with our team. It always seemed to help release the tension that would build up prior to a key match.

We were about to begin a training session when Gary Sprake and Norman Hunter decided to play a practical joke on one of the players. Hunter knelt behind the player while Sprake pushed him over. The trick worked!

Unfortunately, our assistant coach Syd Owen was not amused by the incident. On the contrary, he was angered by it. He verbalized his frustration to the pranksters, telling them that they could have injured their teammate.

The team then proceeded to warm up for the match by jogging around the complex. Friendly banter flew back and forth, interrupted by Owen's continual muttering about the prank.

Sprake, our goalkeeper, then shocked all of us by jumping on Owen's back and pounding him with blows while yelling, "I can't stand it anymore! I've had enough of your moaning!"

We immediately broke up the fray and separated the two men. Sprake was ordered to the manager's office following training.

The incident between Sprake and Owen served a purpose for the club. During the previous weeks, the press had been publishing inside information concerning Leeds United. It was obvious that someone on the staff was leaking sensitive news to the press. The team manager, Don Revie, had addressed the issue with us. We wondered who would do such a thing.

During the scrap that morning, Revie had gone to his office window to see what was happening. That's when he saw one of our injured players who was unable to train run to the telephone box near the club gates. Obviously, the culprit was picking up some extra money from the press.

That player did not remain long at Elland Road. He was soon transferred to another team.

I was shocked to learn that there had been a traitor in our midst, but I've also lived long enough to expect anything from those whose god is money.

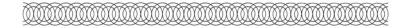

The Glory Years of Leeds United

"For what is your life? It is even a vapor, that appeareth
for a little time, and then vanisheth away."
— JAMES 4:14

The Sunderland game was upon us. Leeds United were at
Roker Park to play one of the hardest games of the grueling
season. Team manager Don Revie had tried to prepare me to
meet stiff opposition in the form of Bobby Kerr, Sunderland's
skilled winger.

This highly talented youngster had already scored 12 goals
on the season, three of them coming in the previous game.
Listening to Revie's instructions, I determined in my mind that
I would shut Kerr out of the game. I convinced myself that not a
single goal would be tallied by this up-and-coming superstar.

The game began and as time ticked by, my confidence
soared. Young Kerr was unable to score. Just three minutes were
left in the 90-minute match when he received the ball. We were
coasting home to a 3-0 victory.

Dutifully following the instructions of our able coaches, I
contained Kerr by guarding him from about two yards away.
I was well aware that the official was ready at any moment to
sound his whistle signaling the end of the game. My heart raced
as I envisioned the sweet victory of the championship.

There was no need to tackle here, I thought. "Simply contain
him." That's when everything suddenly went haywire.

My teammate Norman Hunter, who had been supporting me from behind, lunged at Kerr's legs. Everyone in the stadium heard the sickening sound of breaking bone.

The poor lad struggled to stand up on one good leg as he called for the stretcher.

I turned to Hunter in a fury, "What are you doing?!" I yelled.

"We have to finish the game with a shutout," was his reply.

I knew in my heart that this sorry incident could cost this young rising star his future.

This was uncharacteristic of Hunter. He is a great fellow. He is unassuming and not at all violent. The blame did not lie with him. It rested on the coaches who allowed young players to behave in such a ruthless manner on the pitch.

In the end, the hunter becomes the hunted as players develop records of violent conduct. During my time as a coach and manager, I never condoned this kind of behavior.

I often heard the great Jack Charlton echo my sentiments in the dressing room. Charlton became a world-class player, but I always knew that he had the utmost respect for all of his opponents.

I know that there are many others like Charlton, but how sad that all players cannot at least respect their opponents enough to ensure that their careers are not put in jeopardy by one foolish act. What happened to the game?

International soccer back in those days was full of all kinds of surprises. A match in Leipzig, East Germany, was no different.

We entered the Olympic Stadium there to battle for continued success in the Fairs Cup competition of the top European clubs. It was a mid-week game. The ground was in wretched condition, covered in ice.

The ground crew had worked diligently to break up the glassy surface without much success. Normally, a field in this condition would dictate an automatic cancellation of the match. But since Leeds United had traveled such a long way to compete in this contest, the officials granted permission for the match to begin.

The first half resembled a comedy film with contestants sliding and falling all over the field. Somehow, we managed to survive to halftime with a scoreless tie. We were all freezing and looking forward to the inevitable warming cup of British tea.

Unfortunately, we had not taken into account the deviousness of our opponents. Both teams entered their respective elevators to go to their dressing rooms for the obligatory team talk and some much-needed warm drink.

As we huddled together while shivering in the elevator, it occurred to us that we were not moving, at least not briskly. Our elevator crawled at a snail's pace.

We eventually emerged at our destination, only to be met by officials who told us that we must immediately return to the field for the second half. No warm drink, no organized rallying, no halftime pep talk — just another slow journey back to the frozen tundra.

When the final whistle blew, we had managed to eek out a 1-0 victory. Rejoicing over our win, we soon forgot the elevator incident.

Two years later, however, the great Arsenal Club of England played at that same stadium. To no one's surprise, Arsenal received the same cold welcome as Leeds.

Had the elevator been broken for two years? I doubt it.

Leeds United were locked in a battle against Fullham. Our team was in the running for both the Fairs Cup and the League Championship.

Leeds was always known for having some colorful characters on its team. There were so many talented players who all had their own ideas of how the game should be played. The Revie Machine, as we were called, was in full swing.

Two of our most talented players were Jack Charlton and Bobby Collins. Charlton stood six-foot-two. Collins was barely five feet. Charlton was a very controlled player. Collins was a player who bustled around, causing havoc in midfield and beyond.

I truly believe that the so-called "Glory Years of Leeds" owed much to our team's perfectly drilled defense. Collins was the team captain, so he gave the orders to the rest of us. Revie always told the defenders to gather the ball, and then pass it to a player who could create attacking opportunities for our team.

We always knew what Revie meant by this. It was not a derogatory statement to his players, even though it sounded like one: "Just give it to the lads that can play."

Revie said this not to berate or belittle us, but simply because he wanted Leeds to be on the offensive attack as quickly as possible.

During the Fullham match, Charlton played as he always did. Instead of passing the ball to the nearest "creative" player, which usually was Collins, Charlton would lob the ball downfield. The ball would often end up out of play at the opposite end of the field.

On one such occasion, Collins yelled at Charlton, "You can't play! You can't even deliver a short pass!"

To our astonishment, both players then began to yell at each other. The next thing I knew, Charlton yanked Collins off the ground and began to shake him. It was actually a comical sight to behold, as Charlton shook Collins like a rag doll.

"I've had enough of your moaning!" Charlton yelled.

Collins responded by spitting in Charlton's face.

The two men ended up on the ground scrapping with one another while the game played on. Norman Hunter and I had to pull them apart.

Thank goodness the ball was still in the Fullham half.

When everyone calmed down, Charlton's nose needed some medical attention.

Cooler heads prevailed, thankfully, in the post-game locker room as Charlton and Collins shook hands and resumed their friendship.

Two years later, Johnny Giles took Collins' place in midfield. Revie instructed Charlton the way he always had: "Give Giles the ball when you win it at the back."

Guess what? Charlton stubbornly continued to play the long ball while Giles muttered his discontent — but only at a safe distance.

I learned then that it often takes contrasting styles to forge a cohesive team, even though at times those disparate styles of play may temporarily alienate teammates.

Leeds was blessed to have more than its fair share of gifted and colorful players. Charlton and Collins were two of the all-time best, and both went on to represent their country in a way that made me proud to play alongside them and to call them my friends — even if one of them had to suffer a bloody nose along the way.

Every Scottish player dreams of playing for his native country against England. My opportunity to win this honor arrived one evening when Leeds United was scheduled to play West Bromwich Albion.

I knew that both the Scottish and English team managers were in attendance at this local derby match. Needless to say, I was determined to win a coveted spot on the Scottish national team. I knew that I needed to play well that day.

The international match between Scotland and England was scheduled to take place in three weeks. Representing my country against Brazil and Portugal had been a thrill, but to compete against England would mean the fulfillment of my ultimate desire.

My teammate, Billy Bremner, and I both knew that we were playing to convince John Prentice, the Scottish national team manager, that we were the best choices for his team.

The game deadlocked 20 minutes into the first half when our captain, Bobby Collins, delivered a lengthy pass that found me clear on the left side. I was positioned 20 yards from the West

Bromwich corner flag. I collected the ball even as I spotted the blue and white shirt of a defender closing in on me.

In an instant, my mind raced, "Should I take the chance and shoot for goal?" It was a wet evening, I thought, and the goalkeeper would find it difficult to stop a hard shot.

I took the shot with the utmost confidence. As I watched the ball slip off the goalkeeper's hands into the net, I thought, "You've done it, Bill! You will play for your country against England!"

My teammates were elated as they embraced me, but their happiness couldn't match my own. We won the match that day, 1-0.

After the game in the Leeds dressing room, the Scottish manager came to meet Don Revie, our coach. Following the formalities, Prentice came straight to me and said, "Well done, Willie. Great game. I will see you in three weeks."

We both knew what he meant. I had been selected to play for Scotland.

My joy was short-lived, however, as just one week later the Scottish Football Association fired Prentice. When the final roster was announced for Scotland vs. England, I was not a member of the team. The new manager of Scotland had opted to choose a team comprised mainly of players who played for Scottish teams.

I never did play against England. Life has since taught me that there are greater dreams to pursue.

Superstition has always been a part of soccer, but Don Revie was one of the most superstitious people I knew. Before our games, Revie insisted that he be the one to massage both Norman Hunter and me. Revie also wore the same suit every game as long as we won. If we lost, he would change to a different suit.

Leeds was in Valencia, Spain, to play in a UEFA Cup game against the Valencia team. Two of our key players had been injured the week before.

Passing the hotel hairdressing salon and seeing a stylist free, I decided to stop in and have a haircut. I was sitting in the chair when Revie passed by and then stopped to do a double-take.

"What do you think you are doing?" he asked with a look of consternation.

"Having a trim," I said.

"Willie, that is very bad luck!" Revie said.

I knew that he was already worried about the game due to our team being down two injured players. Seeing me get my hair trimmed right before the match only made matters worse for him. He left shaking his head.

When we lined up for the match, I knew that we had to find a way to win in order to prove Revie's superstition regarding my harmless haircut wrong. When the match ended, we left the pitch with another victory notched in our belts. Leeds won by one goal that night.

No one was happier about the outcome than me. I was not looking forward to being blamed for putting a hex on our team. Even though I wasn't superstitious, that would be the last haircut I would ever receive on match day.

Leeds played the first leg of the Fairs Cup at Elland Road against Uzpest Doza. Although Uzpest was known to be a top-flight team in Hungary, we virtually destroyed them in the first round at Elland Road, our home ground, by a score of 4-0.

Who could touch us with a lead like that heading into our away match in Hungary? So we traveled to Hungary in a very confident mood.

Upon arrival, we entered the field to find the Uzpest Stadium packed with supporters of the Hungarian side. The atmosphere was electric. I could not understand it. With their team already down four goals, it seemed incredible that so many fans would turn out in an attempt to cheer their team on to an improbable comeback against the mighty Leeds United from England.

As I warmed up for the match, I realized that my opponent, No. 7, was a young kid. He looked like he was all of 17 years old.

Our players began saying, "This is a different team. They are a bunch of kids." We were guessing that the Uzpest team, knowing they could not win, were throwing a bunch of youngsters at us like sacrificial lambs. I looked forward to an easy game.

The match kicked off. We were no sooner into play when I realized that this was not the Hungarians' B squad; This was their best team. I can truly say that it was the most challenging match I ever played. It was as if we were chasing shadows.

Uzpest hit the goal post four times in the first half. We could not contain them. Midway through the second half, completely against the run of play, we scored a goal. Immediately, the stadium began to empty.

We won the match that day by a score of 1-0. As we recovered in our dressing room, we learned that the team that had just played us were considered security risks. If the players had been older, with families to care for, the Communist Party rulers in Hungary knew they would be unlikely candidates to seek political asylum in another country.

A brilliant team of players had been kept back in Hungary strictly for political reasons.

I was thankful that I belonged to a country where the government allowed me the freedom to roam the world. I was pleased that we won the game, but angry and frustrated for the highly talented young men who were not allowed to represent their homeland on foreign soil.

Leeds United traveled to Amsterdam to play a match. We had just won and earned a place in the semifinals of the Fairs Cup. Our team had a free evening to spend as we wished. So we decided to head out for dinner at a local restaurant. The next few hours passed by pleasantly as we celebrated the game and savored our victory.

Following our meal, we decided to go for a walk. A light rain began to fall at twilight. I was feeling on top of the world.

Just then, my eye caught a moving figure in the water on the opposite side of the canal which ran alongside the road. My first thought was that it must be a dog.

The figure came to the surface again, and I came to the awful realization that it was a man struggling for his life. I looked for the nearest bridge as my teammates began to discuss a way to rescue this person in great distress.

There was no bridge in the immediate vicinity. We discussed the option of someone swimming out to rescue the struggling man in the water while others reached out from the steep bank in an attempt to pull both men out.

Several of my colleagues couldn't swim and we stood there with an ominous air hanging around us as we watched the poor soul slip into eternity.

I knew in my heart that if it had been a family member in the water, I would have dived in regardless of the cost. However, each of us chose to stand by and watch. The vision of that helpless man still haunts me to this day.

The next day, we read in the local newspaper of an American sailor who had been stabbed and then thrown into the canal.

Our victory on the soccer field in Amsterdam seemed suddenly hollow.

Since becoming a Christian, I have often thought back to that day and wondered whether that poor soul knew he was destined for Heaven.

All in all, my nine years at Leeds were about as rewarding as a young man could hope for — two league championships, an FA Cup Final appearance, two caps for the Scottish National Team, and several trips to the European Championships.

In 260 total appearances at all levels, I registered 18 goals and countless memories.

After I retired, a group of historians who followed Leeds

named me to the Top 100 Players in the history of Club —
alongside such legends as Jack Charlton, Bobby Collins, Norman
Hunter and Billy Bremner.

Ironically, they said that on a team known for its hard-
tackling style of play, I was known as "the hardest of them all."

I'll take that as high praise.

The only thing I regret about my time at Leeds United was
my departure.

Don Revie called me into his office one day and asked if
I would coach the reserve team. When I told him that I still
wanted to play, he looked me squarely in the eye and said that he
had arranged for my sale to Sunderland.

I refused to go. Instead, I insisted that he place my transfer
in the papers and let me seek a playing opportunity at a club of
my own choosing. That's when I went to Leicester City.

Joining Leicester City from Leeds United was a chapter in
my life that lingers. I was joining a club with great tradition.
Manager Matt Gillies was a true gentleman. He was an
administrator, not a coach, but a man in whom you could have
complete trust.

Unfortunately, my stay at the club was cut short by
circumstances that almost gave me a nervous breakdown.

Let me take you back to a time when the club was in a bad
position. Lying in the bottom half of the league table, we had
just lost a crucial match away from home, with the possibility of
relegation on the horizon.

The team had just finished their meals in the dining car on
a train on the way home from another defeat. The players were
gathered in a railway compartment discussing the match.

As I entered, two of our top players were leading a discussion
about the way the coaches were handling the team. The team
coach, Bert Johnstone, was the target. He had been at Leicester
City long before I arrived. This was a first division club with a
proud tradition.

My background at Leeds had been very good as far as coaching goes. Being new to Leicester City, I enjoyed the freedom given to players. In the past, that had given the club wonderful success in the FA Cup.

But now two senior players for Leicester were complaining openly to the younger players about the set-up. They did not like the coach.

As I sat listening to Bobby Roberts and David Gibson, both fellow Scots, complaining, I decided I needed to speak up. As team captain, I said I would ask manager Matt Gillies for a team meeting to allow everyone to express their feelings and ideas.

I thought this might clear the air and give the team a much-needed boost. I went to the dining area and asked Gillies if the players could meet and have an open discussion that could help the club.

His reply was, "Of course, Willie. That is a good idea. Tell the lads that we will meet tomorrow at 11:00 a.m. Sunday in the board room at the stadium." Gillies was very open to my suggestion.

As I left the house Sunday morning, Mary said, "Bill, I hope you will not be disappointed."

In the board room, sitting around the large table were the first team squad and the coach, Bert Johnstone. I was seated at Gillies' left side. He proceeded to tell us that whatever would be discussed would not be held against anyone.

From his right, one by one, much of the same answers came forth. "Soon, we will put it all together," the players said.

I expected the young players to hold back. When he came to Roberts and Gibson, both players said, "We feel that it is only a matter of time; things will get better."

They dismissed everything they had spoken about. I could not believe what I was hearing.

Next, Peter Shilton was asked the same questions. He was an international goalkeeper for England and one of the best in the world. He was the only player who spoke up. He said that we were not professional enough as a team. He said we did not know enough about the opposition. He was constructive in his comments.

Eventually, Gillies turned to me. My answer was, "I cannot captain this team. If we don't speak up in here, how can we play in front of thousands?"

Gillies closed the meeting and thanked us all for coming. He pulled me aside and said, "Willie, I know who is behind this; it has happened before. Who do you think could be captain?"

I said. "The only person I feel who is qualified is David Nish."

Nish became captain of Leicester City from that point on.

The following week, I took the flu and was at home while the team was going to play Everton. I went into our facilities to do some light training. I was approached by Gibson and Roberts in the dressing room. Both said to me, "Would you come with us this afternoon to a meeting with the Chairman?"

My answer was, "No — you had your chance — and you kept your mouth shut." I went home.

Leicester City had fired Bert Johnstone. That was the news on the TV the night before Leicester played Everton at Goodison Park. They were going to play Everton without a coach. The news also said that Matt Gillies would be resigning. Everton won by six goals, and I was absolutely stunned.

Monday morning came around and I once gain came in to do some light training. Filbert Street was the name of the Leicester City stadium then. The car park was empty. The players were given Monday off after the disastrous result on Saturday.

As I entered the stadium, the secretary said, "Mr. Gillies would like to see you in his office." I went into his office to meet with him.

He asked me if I would coach the club while he conducted a search for a new coach. I asked him if he would stay too. He said no. Gillies also said that I could not play and coach. He just wanted me to coach.

Tuesday morning, as I came back in, Gillies took me to the training ground to introduce me as the new coach. Gillies asked the players to come in and join the indoor session. He explained that I would be taking over the team until a new manager was appointed.

When he left, I stood there and said, "I guess you read the papers over the weekend."

The next game, the next Saturday, we played Manchester United at home. It was my first game as coach at Leicester City. I asked for the latest film of Manchester United. I had no match reports, and I needed film from the television.

I brought the team back and we watched the film. I told the team the tactics we would use. The tactics worked and we beat United 1-0. Coming off the field, Matt Busby, the legendary United manager, came over and said, "Willie, you did a wonderful job." I thanked him for his kind words.

We played another game and managed to get a tie. Then we had a friendly match in Germany with our sister city — Kaiserslautern. We were to play them at their home park.

The atmosphere at the club was wonderful. We had secured two good results.

I was in Germany having a pre-match meal with the team, excited about the game, and in walked one of the directors with the new appointed manager, Frank O'Farrell.

O'Farrell came over and sat beside me. He asked me how the team was doing. I told him they were working hard but had a long way to go.

He said he wanted me to be the head coach and continue doing what I was doing. He said I was doing a good job.

He also said, "I would like you to play tonight at left back." I said, "I haven't been training as hard as the players," but I played nonetheless.

We did quite well that night. The team performed at a high level.

We then traveled back to England for a game against Burnley away from home.

We traveled there on the team bus, and the atmosphere was great. He put me in the team to play at left back.

The day of the match, I was in the dressing room as we were getting ready for the game.

In walked O'Farrell into the dressing room. He came in with another coach, Malcolm Musgrove. O'Farrell told the players, "I want you to meet your new head coach."

All eyes turned to me. I just kept my head down. I didn't know what to do. That was my last first-team game for Leicester City. After that, I was put on the second team. It was just a terrible shock. Nobody knew it was happening.

While playing for the reserve team, I knew I was a more experienced player than the left back who was playing on the first team. I told O'Farrell that I knew I could help the team, but he did not listen to me.

Sure enough, the team started to lose games. At practice one day, the first team was going to play the second team. O'Farrell came onto the field and called my name before the match.

He told me that I would play with the first team. I told him, "No chance." I never played again for Leicester City.

When it came to the end of the season, I was given a free transfer to go anywhere I wanted. I watched Leicester get relegated to the second division.

I learned a lot from that experience about management and coaching. It was a growing experience, but it was a difficult time in my life.

When I look back at my time at Leicester City, I realize that I never got any support from the directors there. Nobody ever came to me.

It becomes part of the job, but it shouldn't be that way. There should be representation for managers and coaches. The players have a union, but the coaches and managers have no one to defend them. They are fighting a losing battle.

Albert Johannson: My Next Door Neighbor

The sound of bongo drums filled the neighborhood around West Lea Gardens as if to say, "Leeds United won!"

This was the way that forward Albert Johannson would celebrate the Yorkshire Club's victory. On rare occasions, the beat would be slow and melancholy when they lost. With windows wide open, the African winger's mood would be known to all.

When he arrived in Yorkshire from Africa, the supporters greeted the young striker with open arms. Within months, a proud, black South African could be seen behind the wheel of a large, bright-red car. Johannson later married a wonderful Jamaican woman, Norma, who would become the mother of two lovely children.

The early days allowed Johannson to play and gain confidence against second division players before eventually facing elite competition in the premier division. His performance would always be "just enough" to please the home crowd. Occasionally, Don Revie would replace him with Terry Cooper if Revie felt the opposing defense was too physical for Johannson.

I can still see Johannson juggling the ball even while the game was in progress, but only during home matches. Away from home, Johannson did not want to get involved. He needed his hometown supporters.

Fortunately for manager Revie, his organized warriors could survive without No. 11 on the pitch. But during our time together, I would always encourage Johannson to take on the opponent's fullback. I would say, "Just take the man on. Run him. Show him that you are better than he is."

Johannson's moods affected his family — so much that his wife was forced to leave home for good. Two years of inconsistency came to a head at Wembley. In the 1965 F.A. Cup Final, Leeds United were missing two key players — Jim Storrie and Albert Johannson. Storrie was injured. Johannson was missing.

That proved to be Johannson's swan song for Leeds. I would

learn later that there were days when Johannson would sit for hours in the Turkish baths in Leeds while recovering from a drinking binge.

All of this was going on without the club officials or other players knowing about it. How sad that no one in Johannson's family ever told Revie or one of the striker's teammates about the athlete's problem. He was even forced to sell his medals to support his alcohol addiction.

While visiting England a few years ago, I read a small article in the national newspaper: "Albert Johannson found dead in a derelict house in Leeds."

What a tragic loss. Had we known the true depths of his personal problems, someone on our club could have reached out and helped him.

Leeds United vs. Derby County: What Price Glory?

During my first season playing with the first team for Leeds United, we traveled to the baseball ground at Derby, always known as a very tough place to play.

As the players prepared in the dressing room prior to the match, I overheard two of our forwards talking about Mathewson, the opposing goalkeeper.

"We must watch ourselves if we have a one-on-one with him. He will kill us if given the chance," they said.

I chuckled at their banter, but I still tucked that helpful piece of information away in my head.

Midway through the second half, a long pass was played to Leeds forward Noel Peyton. I started my run with hopes that he would spot me — and he did.

At just the right moment, Peyton opened his legs and "dummied" the ball so that it would carry clean to my position some 40 yards from goal.

I was in, with nothing but Mathewson between the goal and me. Approaching the goal at full speed, I saw the goalkeeper sprinting toward me like a bat out of hell.

At the last possible moment, I toe-poked the ball past the keeper and lifted both of my legs off the ground. The next thing I felt was this thunderous keeper striking me flush above the knees and spinning me around in the air.

The collision that my teammates had predicted before the match had come true. Only this time, the keeper forgot to stop something else very important: the ball.

When I came back to earth, I saw the most beautiful sight in the world — a soccer ball nestled safely in the back corner of the net. Goal!

A jubilant Leeds United team pulled me up so that I could stand on my wobbly legs.

To this day, I can still hear my teammate Grenville Hairs' voice as he grabbed my arms: "That was a four-pounds bonus goal, Willie!"

Ironically, that was the last thing on my mind.

Leeds United vs. Chelsea: F.A. Cup Semifinal, 1967

Villa Park hosted the semifinals for the F.A. Cup in 1967. Win there, and we would be off to Wembley to compete for the F.A. Cup Championship for the second year in a row.

The previous year, we had lost in the final to Liverpool in extra time. Our Leeds team that season was young and inexperienced, but we were fighters.

This time, versus Chelsea, we fielded a more mature outfit. Still, Chelsea were considered the solid favorites to win the coveted trophy.

Tommy Docherty's Chelsea Football Club had a few highly talented players capable of turning matches, and on this day they did just that.

With Leeds trailing 3-2 and the clock winding down, Chelsea was frantically defending against an all-out onslaught by our team. With just minutes left in the match, we were awarded an indirect free kick about 20 yards from goal.

We knew this might be out last scoring chance of the day.

We also knew that we had a few good set pieces planned for exactly this kind of situation.

In this instance, the responsibility for the play rested squarely on the shoulders of Peter Lorimar. The official took plenty of time — what seemed to be an eternity — to push back the Chelsea wall the requisite 10 yards from the ball.

Chelsea knew that Lorimar had one of the strongest shots in the game, and they weren't going to budge even a half-inch more than they absolutely had to.

The wall was to no avail. Lorimar's cracker of a shot struck the back of the Chelsea net with a thunderous and ferocious crash. Goal!

The white army of Leeds United celebrated by jumping all over Lorimar in wild glee.

Our triumph lasted all of 20 seconds, however, as the official informed us that we had to retake the kick.

Center referee Burns was immediately bombarded by our collective protests. But he would have none of it. A Chelsea player had encroached and the referee had stopped play just before the shot.

Lorimar's second shot proved harmless, and we lost the match.

Referee Burns never made it to the final. Neither did Leeds.

Leeds United vs. Everton: The Most Frightening Game I Ever Played In

We arrived for match day at Goodison Park, home field of the famed Everton Football Club. Again, it was a day in which our opponent would give its best effort toward stopping the runaway freight train that had become Leeds United.

But more than this was at stake. Everyone knew that there was little friendship between the two clubs.

Jack Charlton won the kickoff and decided to play a long ball deep into the Everton half. That's when the match suddenly exploded.

Roy Vernon, the Everton forward, decided to go for the big man Charlton's legs. Instantly, the referee stopped the match and booked Vernon with a yellow card.

One minute later, Johnny Giles received a pass on the right wing and pushed it past Everton fullback Sandy Brown. The defender then proceeded to punch Giles in the stomach.

Brown was immediately issued a red card by the referee and sent off — but the rest of us still on the field were left to wonder: What would happen next?

For the next 40 minutes, tackles became increasingly vicious. The center referee completely lost control of the match.

A long, cross-field ball was played to Everton right winger John Temple. I had a good chance of winning the ball inside the opponent's half. The next thing I remember, both Temple and I were lying on the ground following a violent collision.

I ached down one entire side of my body as I looked over at Temple, who remained motionless on the grass.

Les Crocker, the Leeds trainer, was the first to see me. "What's hurting, Willie?" he said.

"I'm OK. Just stunned a bit," I said.

"Don't move," Crocker replied. "If you do, the referee will send you off."

I obliged. As I was carried off the field, I saw that all of the players had been taken off the field by the official.

In the dressing room, the officials lectured both teams, warning us that one more infringement would mean suspension for both teams and possibly a deduction of points.

The game restarted, minus Everton's right winger.

The referee's final whistle came as a welcome relief that day. Leeds United won the match, 1-0. I had scored the only goal of the game.

Sunday morning's papers covered the "Battle at Goodison" with nary a mention of my game-winning goal. But they did feature a picture of me being carried off the field.

It's a shame that bad news sells newspapers. The goals are the best part of the game, but who wants to read about goals when you can sell the violence of the sport?

The press took an ugly game and made it uglier.

Leeds United vs. Manchester United: Chasing the Championship

Two of the most storied clubs in the history of British football — Leeds United and Manchester United — were locked in a tie at the top of the division, separated only by goal differential. The tie-breaking match would be played at the hallowed grounds of Manchester United: at packed and sacred Old Trafford.

The stakes were so high, the match even received its own title: "The Battle of the Roses."

A very young but talented Leeds United, promoted only the previous year into the first division, would battle it out for a possible chance of pulling off the proverbial double — another league championship.

It was a typical March day in England, starting off with a light fog as we traveled over the hills separating Yorkshire and Lancashire. We were all set for "The Big One."

The atmosphere surrounding this match was tremendous. Thousands of red and white scarves mingled with the all-white scarves and gear of Leeds United.

Shortly after kickoff, the flood lights were engaged. Visibility on the grounds was not very good, but that did not prevent Leeds from getting on the scoreboard first.

Just 15 minutes from the final whistle, Leeds United tallied an all-important goal. But could we hold on? The Reds were rallying to their supporters' cries — and then it happened again.

The fog began to roll over the Stratford Road end of the stadium, making its way across the field. From my position at fullback, I could not even see my team's forwards.

All of the players knew that the match officials would have to make a decision soon. When the whistle blew to stop play, both teams headed for their dressing rooms.

Standing at the tunnel, Matt Busby, the legendary manager

of Manchester United, smiled as we shuffled in toward the lockers. "Don't worry, lads. It may lift," he said in his broad Scottish accent.

Just at that moment, Don Revie, the Leeds United manager, responded: "It is OK for you to smile," he said. "I bet you are happy that the game's been stopped." Revie's emotions were evident. It's a pity he felt he had to address a gentleman like Busby in such a manner.

Ten minutes later, both teams entered the field of play again. The fog had lifted. Leeds United continued to hold out, leaving Old Trafford with a huge victory and hard-earned points in the standings.

Still, I somehow felt that the tunnel incident had left a bad taste in Old Trafford.

A good win marred by bad blood.

Leeds United vs. Sunderland: Set Piece

I still remember the afternoon inside Sunderland's Roker Park dressing room. The usual routines took place. Leeds United's Don Revie was the most routine of all.

Very superstitious, one of his rituals was to rub our backs with wintergreen just before leaving the dressing room. Of course, with the November weather quite chilly, the application of warm wintergreen was more than welcomed.

One routine was to discuss strategy. Bobby Collins, Jack Charlton, Billy Bremner and I were discussing the deadball situations we had practiced during the week when Revie interrupted and asked us to gather around the table in the middle of the room.

He proceeded to set up drinking cups to represent a defensive wall. He then told Bremner and Collins to look for me darting behind the Sunderland wall.

Charlton and I would normally take the backpost position on set pieces, but on this day Revie felt that Sunderland would be prepared to defend against this tactic.

"Let's see if we can get Willie in as he begins to go off the ball behind the wall when Billy goes over the ball," said Revie.

The plan would take effect with Bobby coming behind Billy, who would then chip the ball over the defensive wall.

Some 25 minutes into the match, Leeds United was awarded a free kick just 25 yards from goal. The scene was set. Collins and Bremner indicated that the ball was being sent toward the back post. Sunderland set their defensive alignment accordingly.

Once Bremner ran over the ball, I took off. Collins' chip over the wall was perfectly placed for me to strike a volley.

As I looked toward the Sunderland goal, I was still airborne after connecting with the pass from Collins. I saw the goalkeeper grasping the air while the ball I struck settled into the net.

This was probably the best goal I ever scored during my career. Leeds United won that match, and yet we never used that set play again.

Maybe Revie was too superstitious to think that it would work more than once.

The Game Within a Game

Match day in British soccer is a day like none other. Passionate fan bases line up to scream out their lungs while young men battle for their club, their community, their pride, and most of all, their professional lives.

Often, this combination of pageantry, passion and pride adds up to form a combustible mix of emotion.

Against Manchester City, this emotion boiled over.

This would be the event that would mark my second and final caution from a referee.

A throw-in was awarded to Manchester City under the stands at Ellan's Road. The ball was thrown to Mike Somerbee, the Manchester right winger who would later star in the classic Sylvester Stallone soccer film, "Victory."

I positioned myself behind Somerbee and headed the ball back out of play. As I stayed close to Somerbee, he called out to his coach, Malcolm Allison, sitting on the team bench, "This guy is a (bleep)!"

Not only did his coach hear the remark, but so did everyone in the Manchester City stands on that side of the field.

My stomach turned as anger burned inside of me. I said nothing.

Upon the next throw-in, I decided to challenge Somerbee for the ball directly. Waiting until he controlled the ball, I kicked him across the knees.

Looking down at him, I asked, "Who's a (bleep)?"

A yellow card for me. A black and blue leg for my opponent.

On a practice day, we were engaged in a shooting session as manager Taylor's new signee, Tommy Murray arrived by taxi.

The Scottish forward had been acquired from Queen of the South in Scotland to help our front line score more goals. As the taxi pulled off, a stray ball bobbled near Murray.

He quickly picked it up. Being a skilled player, his return volley displayed pinpoint accuracy. As the ball cleared the fence, all eyes fixated squarely on Leeds United's new star.

The internal celebration proved premature, however, as we quickly learned that Murray had pulled a thigh muscle by demonstrating his kicking brilliance.

Without even joining our squad for practice, he limped off the field and went straight to the trainer's facility. It would be four full weeks before Murray could suit up for our club for the first time.

Hail the conquering hero.

Burnley, here we come. It was time for the annual pilgrimage of Leeds United to Lancashire, England, for a Rose's Battle — the away match versus Burnley.

As always, a full house would be guaranteed. In the dressing room, Don Revie reminded us that Blacklaw, the Burnley goalkeeper, might be vulnerable to long shots. Revie shared that he had heard that the keeper's eyesight was suspect.

It was a bright, sunny day when both teams were introduced to Field Marshall Montgomery, known to all in Great Britain affectionately as Monty after his successful campaign in Africa against Rommel during World War II.

The game turned into a typical local derby, close and hotly contested.

On a possession Leeds once again pressed the attack hard at the Burnley defense. I found myself open just inside our opponents' half and quickly received a pass from midfielder Norman Hunter.

I was moving forward about 35 yards from the Burnley goal when I fired the ball with my left foot. Blacklaw saw it too late as the ball rocketed into the upper left-hand corner of the goal.

The next thing I knew, Billy Bremner was in my arms, followed quickly by Hunter. That afternoon, Leeds United achieved a great result.

Was it my shot that was special that day, or was it simply the goalkeeper's poor eyesight that made my winning goal look so good?

Whatever the reason, the long shot proved to be the difference that day, and I will always have Coach Revie to thank for giving me that timely pre-game tip.

My Last Game for Leeds United

Unknown to me, the match against Nottingham Forest was to be my final game suiting up for Leeds United.

We were beating Nottingham Forest at Elland Road, 2-0, and all was going well. I had scored a goal on a header off a corner kick. Our team captain, Bobby Collins, tallied a goal too.

Then it happened. Keith Newton, Forest midfielder, attempted to shoot on goal from 20 yards out. My first thought was to block the shot. My right leg, outstretched, enabled me to stop the ball with my toe.

That's when I felt my knee joint open. Down I went, in a heap. Within seconds, team trainer Les Cocker called for the stretcher to carry me off the field.

My wife, Mary, joined us in the dressing room. She had seen the incident and feared the worst.

Three weeks passed and rehabilitation began to show some good results. I felt like I was ready to compete again. The team trainer cleared me to play after I passed a fitness test.

Unfortunately, Don Revie had other ideas. When he announced the squad for the Queens Park Rangers match, he omitted my name. Instead, I heard, "Willie, will you come back with me to the stadium?"

The short ride back to Leeds allowed Revie to tell me that he would like me to play and help coach the second team. He felt that my input would be invaluable to the club.

Then, I said what he wanted to hear — that I was too good to play for the second team and that perhaps it was time for me to leave Leeds United after nine years with the club.

"Well, I know Sunderland would buy you tomorrow if you would like to go," he said.

It all began to fit together. The purchase of Mick Jones had put Revie further in the red. I was the obvious pawn.

On Monday morning, I entered Revie's office, quickly telling him that I was ready to leave.

"Do you want to speak to Sunderland?" Revie asked.

"No. Just put my transfer in the newspapers and then I will make a decision," I said.

That was the last time I spoke to Revie about his arrangement with Sunderland. By Tuesday, Leicester City had called to invite Mary and me to visit.

I was on my way.

Bobby Collins: A Legend Goes to Glory

My early days with Leeds United's "Revie Machine" were filled with a lot of success largely due to the presence of one of the best players of all time — Bobby Collins.

He was always known as a skillful and tenacious team

captain. He had been a top player with Glasgow Celtic and Everton before coming to Leeds, and he was still in his prime when he and I were teammates.

His influence was immense, as he led Leeds United to begin its decade of dominance and usher in the glory years of Don Revie's highly touted squad.

Collins was short, stocky and a player's player. Defeat was simply not an option for him. He was voted player of the year when Leeds finished second by a single point to Manchester United in the league standings and runner-up in the European Fairs Cup. He also played for the Scottish national team.

What happened during a game in Turin, Italy, spoke volumes about this man's character. I had been injured the previous week in a game against Sunderland, but I traveled with the team to Turin for a Fairs Cup match.

It was a warm evening. Leeds United was the better team, and Collins was running the show from his normal midfield position. A throw-in taken by Norman Hunter was collected by Collins. As he pushed the ball past a Turin defender, the Italian player lifted his knee and caught Collins on the thigh.

Collins spun in the air, hit the ground and then remained motionless on the pitch while the team trainer Les Crocker quickly ran across the field to tend to him.

The news was bad. Collins had broken the bone in his thigh. I told both Revie and Crocker that I would go with Collins to the hospital.

On the way to the hospital, Collins asked me to tell the ambulance driver to slow down because his thigh was experiencing excruciating pain. I tried to comfort him by saying, "Bobby, you are going to be OK. The injury is on your left leg, and you have a great right foot."

Collins replied, "I still have to stand on my left (bleep-bleep) leg!"

At that point, we both laughed.

In the hospital emergency room, the doctor examined

Collins' leg and immediately prepared to give him an injection to ease the pain.

With a large grin, Collins winked at me and then let out a very loud yell, which shook the doctor so much that he fell backward. As soon as we realized the good-natured joke that Collins had just played on everyone, we all just laughed.

A few months later, Collins was back to his normal self, dominating play on the field.

In 2010, my wife Mary and I visited Collins during one of our mission trips in England. His dear wife Betty told us of his early Alzheimer's disease. I went on a walk with my good friend Bobby around the neighborhood. It was an opportunity for me to share my faith with him.

The conversation went like this:

"Bobby, have you ever been to America?"

Of course, I knew he had toured America with Glasgow Celtic.

"Yes," he replied. "We went on the Queen Mary."

"When you were with Celtic, did the priests ever speak to the team?"

Bobby didn't hesitate. "Yes, they did."

"Did they ever tell you about Jesus?"

"Yes," he said.

"Do you believe that Jesus died for you on the cross?"

"Oh yes, I believe that," he said.

I was very happy for my friend and thankful that we had that conversation before his mind totally slipped away.

In February of 2014, my dear friend entered glory. I believe that he heard his Savior say, "Welcome into the joy of the Lord."

I know that one day I will see Bobby again. Will you?

"If you confess with your mouth and believe in your heart that God has raised Jesus from the dead, you will be saved."

— ROMANS 10:9

Leeds United returns home to a warm welcome from their supporters in Leeds, England, following the team's FA Cup Final loss to Liverpool at Wembley Stadium in 1965. Leeds United completed a remarkable year in which the club finished as runners-up in the FA Cup, the League

Championship (by one point to Manchester United), and the Fairs Cup (following a loss in the final to Zaragosa, Spain). Bell can be seen at top left, his face partially obscured by the street pole.

ii

Bell scores a goal that would ultimately be disallowed versus Manchester United in the FA Cup Semifinal. While Bell's header was called back, his Leeds United team would go on to defeat Manchester United 1-0. The legendary Bobby Charlton can be seen at the far left of this classic photo.

Bell shakes the hand of of Prince Philip, Duke of Edinburgh, prior to the FA Cup Final at Wembley in 1965. Bell's Leeds United club would go on to lose to Liverpool in the game.

Bell coaching his first team at Birmingham City, England.
Around him on the pitch, from left, are Keith Bertschin, Trevor Francis,
Gary Jones, Kevan Broadhurst and John Connolly.

Lincoln City team photo taken at the home grounds of Lincoln City during the
1977-1978 season. This would be Bell's final year of coaching professionally in
England. Bell is seated in the front row, fourth from left.

Birmingham City: Managing the Gauntlet

*"Therefore all things whatsoever ye would that men should do to you,
do ye even so to them: for this is the law and the prophets."*
— MATTHEW 7:12

Faithful supporters — what would we do without them? I spent many evenings at my office as a team manager answering letters from fans. Some of them praised my job at Birmingham City. Others expressed concern.

These special followers spend their hard-earned cash to support their favorite team. They challenge their chosen teams to be the best they can possibly be.

Taking a family to watch a game is a very expensive outing, especially when the family is supported by a blue-collar factory worker. For most British clubs playing in the 1960s and 1970s, factory workers formed the backbone of the crowd. They worked hard every day, and cheered even harder for their beloved team each week.

Whenever a supporter would criticize me as a player, I would respond by saying, "You are entitled to your opinion. You pay my salary."

I never took offense when confronted by a fan. They paid their money to attend the match. And I'd rather they did that. It beat the opposite — playing in front of an empty grandstand, which wouldn't last long.

My first season as manager of Birmingham City was a nightmare. We were third from the bottom of the league in the standings. Our diehard fans, known affectionately as the "Blues," rose to the occasion.

We were playing against Aston Villa, our rivals from the other end of the city. It was an all-ticket affair at Villa Park. A tie would keep the flames of hope burning for our side. A loss would be devastating, as it could tip our hand toward relegation to a lower division.

That day, we played extremely well. We outplayed and outclassed Villa throughout the match. With very little time left on the clock, the desired draw appeared to be securely in hand.

Kenny Burns, our central defender, collected the ball inside our penalty area. The most sensible thing to do was release it swiftly to a teammate. Burns, unfortunately, chose not to be sensible at that moment.

Rather, he decided he would try to beat his opposing player, Brian Little. I could only watch in horror as Little won the ball from Burns and then slotted it into the net for the winning goal.

It seemed so unfair. During my entire tenure as manager of Birmingham City, that was the one and only defeat we suffered to Aston Villa. Our supporters had been so wonderful. They knew their beloved team had given its all, only to experience the most crushing defeat. The fans' disappointment was as great as mine.

During another match at Villa, a 30-yard shot from John Connelly won the game for Birmingham City. The fans literally went wild with sheer joy.

Following the game, I was driving home along the Stratford Road when I was stopped at a traffic light by a fan who was on his knees bowing to my car. He was a man who saw everything blue that night, including my blue Mercedes.

But that was not the most amazing thing I saw. One day, I received a telephone call from a widow requesting that she be allowed to scatter her husband's ashes in the penalty area of the

St. Andrew's ground. That had been her departed husband's wishes.

The lady duly arrived with her family. I stood in the players' tunnel and watched the family carry out the wishes of the deceased supporter. I couldn't quite understand such fervor, but I also knew that supporters like this were the mainstay of our game.

Hooliganism, however, is another story. Too much of British soccer has been marred by boorish behavior over the years. Fans of this ilk are rightly called soccer hooligans.

These are the ones who bring disgrace not only to themselves, but to their team and their country.

It is easy to be brave in a crowd. At Leeds United's home ground, the police would routinely toss the "rowdies," as we called them, into a holding room at the stadium before the game even started. There, they were forced to wash the floor.

Their greatest punishment was having to hear the roar of the crowd above them as the game played on without them. This plan by the police proved to be an effective deterrent to hooliganism at Leeds matches.

All clubs would benefit from such holding areas. But the players themselves could do a lot to avoid contention by behaving better on the field too. Too many times, I have seen the actions of players on the field incite the fans to riotous conduct. How sad. That's how, in 1989 in Sheffield, England, 96 fans were crushed to death.

For the most part, though, teams leave the field the best of friends, while some fans carry their animosity toward the opponents home with them.

I was sitting in my office at Birmingham City's ground when the phone rang. My secretary said, "Mr. Bell, there is a young man here wishing to speak with you."

I wondered who would want to speak with me without an appointment. "Send him in," I responded.

The door opened to reveal a young boy, who appeared to be about 17. "What can I do for you, son?" I asked.

"I have come to tell you as manager of the Blues that I want a tryout. I know I am good enough to play for you. All I need is a chance," the young lad said.

Immediately, my mind flew back to the day I had been so humiliated by the St. Mirren manager when I did exactly what this young man was doing in my office. When I was a lad, the St. Mirren manager dismissed me in an unfeeling manner without even giving me a chance.

"All right, son. You turn up for training on Monday morning at 9:00 a.m. and you can try out for the Blues," I said, disguising the smile that rose to my lips as the youngster looked incredulous.

"Thank you, Mr. Bell," he said excitedly, leaving the office more confident than when he had entered.

It felt good to be able to encourage the lad as I relived the bitter rejection I had experienced those many years ago.

Monday morning arrived. With the week's training about to begin, I met to prepare tactics with my coaching staff. Our equipment manager, Ray Devie, entered to say, "Boss, there is a youngster outside. He says you told him he could try out for the team today."

"That's right," I said. "Put him with the apprentices, give him some gear, and we shall see how he does. I will talk to him later."

Later that day, I emerged from the dressing room. I was the last to leave. My glance caught the young trialist sitting on the bench outside the dressing room. He was laid back, obviously exhausted, puffing on a cigarette.

The boy struggled to sit upright when he saw me.

"Well, son, did you enjoy the morning?" I enquired.

"Yes," came the breathless reply.

"Good for you. Come back tomorrow, and I can have a close look at you then," I said.

The lad never returned. I guess the pace was more than he had anticipated, the professional level too hard for him.

Nevertheless, the young hopeful had fulfilled his desire. He had tried out for the Blues. He could have been a star in the raw, but he was not.

It gives me pleasure to this day to know that I had the opportunity to perhaps right a wrong I had suffered as a young hopeful.

As eventually happens to all managers, I came to the point in my career when I was fired by Birmingham City. Sir Alf Ramsey — who had led England to World Cup glory in 1966 — had joined the board of the club. So, four games into a season in which we lost our center-half with an injury and suffered several losses, it was inevitable that the ex-manager of England would be named to be my replacement.

But there was more to this story — and it began the year before.

The buildup started when the team went golfing to Malvern for a two-day break as a reward for their hard work.

I received a call from Mr. Coombs, the club chairman's brother. He asked if I would take on Sir Alf Ramsey as general manager. Mr. Coombs wanted Ramsey to join the board. "But unless we give him a position, we cannot pay him," Mr. Coombs said to me.

This happened when the team was doing very well. I kept receiving calls from Mr. Coombs. I said it wouldn't look good to bring on the England team manager. He had retired from the England job.

I attended a board meeting four weeks later with the directors of Birmingham City. Ramsey was sitting at the board room table. At the time of that of that meeting somehow he had been placed on the board.

I said to Ramsey, "Look, no disrespect, but do not come into the dressing room before games." We were in the top half of the table and playing very well. One day the chairman came into the dressing room with Ramsey, and Ramsey started to speak to the players. I was against this from the beginning. He thought he had the freedom to come in and discuss things with the players before the game.

A good example of the tension between Ramsey and me came when our star player, Kenny Burns, left the club. I had put him up for sale because of the way he was behaving off the field. He was a bad leader and a bad influence on the other players.

Ramsey tried to keep him. He said to me: "You can't let good players like this go."

I replied, "I can't let a bad influence ruin the whole team."

Ramsey traveled with us to Holland for overseas training at the start of the next season. During our time in Holland, Burns let the club down badly, and Ramsey saw this. When I wanted to sell him, Ramsey opposed me in the board room.

However, I maintained my position. I knew that Burns had been illegally approached by another club. It was time for us to part ways with a player who could no longer be trusted to be loyal and lead our club.

Ramsey saw Burns at his worst off the field. Despite that, Ramsey opposed me and said we can't let a good player like this go. I said, "Players like this will destroy a club."

When we played our first game, it was against Liverpool. We bombarded their goal but we could not score. Kevin Broadhurst and another young player — Jim Calderwood — were put in by me.

After the game, the Birmingham supporters would not leave the stadium until these two young players came back so that the fans could thank them. I got fired the next day.

Ramsey took over the job and just lasted a few months — and then they got rid of him, too.

During my time at Birmingham City, I sold six players and bought three. Ramsey was just sitting there waiting to take my job the whole time. We had laid a good foundation. We were headed in the right direction. But the club directors ruined it.

To this day, I harbor no bitterness over how my coaching situation was handled by the club. Though I had taken the team from the second division to the first division within three years and had coached the team successfully for six years, I understood the rules of the game.

The game teaches one to expect to be the scapegoat when the team is unsuccessful. Birmingham City had been kind enough to let me keep my Mercedes and had given me a few thousand pounds to see me through the next few months.

As the weeks passed, I became restless and anxious to find another position. One day, the telephone rang. Upon answering the call, I heard the voice of Bobby Robson, the Ipswich manager. Robson asked if I would be willing to undertake some scouting jobs for him.

I would be allocated a ticket in the director's box at each game I covered and be paid a generous fee for my efforts. More importantly, however, I would be in touch with the game.

My self-esteem rocketed at Robson's request. This was a lifeline to me, and Robson knew it.

My Saturdays were spent attending games, followed by a written report to Robson each Monday morning. Two days later, I would receive a call in which we discussed the Ipswich opponent whom I had scouted.

I became an avid supporter of Ipswich Town. I felt involved in the team. I can't even fully express what a difference Robson's gesture made in my life. I will be eternally grateful for such a friend.

Many years later, Robson and I met over breakfast in St. Louis, Mo. He told me of the time that he himself had been fired by the Fulham Football Club. It was at Christmas time. Robson had gone into the local TV and radio store to ask the salesman to send a color TV to his home. The television set was intended to be a surprise for his wife and children on Christmas.

"Are you the Bobby Robson who has just been fired by

Fulham?" asked the proprietor of the store. And then, without skipping a beat, he said to his customer, "You can't afford this."

Needless to say, that statement left an indelible mark on Robson's mind and heart. He used the experience to help others in similar situations through the years.

I salute a great man, Bobby Robson, who turned misfortune for himself into a blessing for so many others. Thank you, Bobby Robson.

I went on to manage Lincoln City for a year before ending my professional English Football career on October 23, 1978.

More than two decades of playing and managing on the fields of Scotland and England had prepared me quite well for the next phase of my life.

Little did I know it at the time, but my trek through Neilston Juniors, Queens Park Rangers, Leeds United, Leicester City, Brighton and Hove Albion, Birmingham City and Lincoln City molded every aspect of my thinking about football and how I would coach young men in the future.

Valuable lessons about teamwork, tackling, technique, tactics, recruiting, motivating, training, fitness, management, investment and preparation were imparted to me by Don Revie, Sir Alf Ramsey, Jack Charlton, Bobby Collins, Norman Hunter and many, many others.

I use them to this day.

Lancaster Gate: The Archie Styles Case

Old Trafford, home pitch of Manchester United, hosted a match in which my club, Birmingham City, was under tremendous pressure.

It proved to be the match in which we would lose our left back, Archie Styles, sent off for an infringement against the United right winger.

Styles was having a bad day as the Reds continued to build attack after attack on the right side. A bad tackle by an opposing fullback was followed by Styles standing on his opponent's hand. The official had no option but to send the defender off.

As I'm sitting on the visitors' bench, I watch Styles come toward me enroute to the tunnel. I see him take his gum from his mouth and throw it in disgust onto the track before disappearing into the dressing room.

At the end of the match, I tell Styles that I will make a decision about discipline after the officials' report on his red card incident is put on my desk on Wednesday. I knew one thing for sure: The Football Association would have an automatic two-game suspension handed down to Styles.

On Wednesday, I received the report, along with a request that Styles and myself report to Lancaster Gate, London, on Friday. The report stated that the player committed the infraction as we saw it, but then while walking to the dressing room gave an obscene gesture to the crowd.

I simply thought that the referee had made a mistake in his report. I even called the local TV sports station to request a copy of the incident. No problem, they said.

On Friday, our names were called and we were both summoned into a large room at Lancaster Gate. The entire Football Association Committee was present for the hearing with Styles and me.

"Have a seat," the committee chairman said before going on to read the referee's report, with the referee who filed the report sitting just opposite us.

The chairman read the section in which the referee claimed that Styles gave an obscene gesture to the crowd.

"Have you anything to say, gentlemen?" the chairman asks.

"Yes, I have with me a film of the incident," I said. "I can prove that Archie did not make a gesture toward the crowd."

All of us leave the room and move to another room equipped with a projector. The film showed, very clearly, that the referee was wrong. Sitting back around the table, the chairman asked the referee if he still stood by his report.

"Yes, I do," he said.

I proceeded to say, "You must be joking."

I was told to keep quiet or I would have to leave the room.

Next, one of the two linesmen from the game entered the room. The whole thing was repeated again, including the film replay. The linesman was asked, "Do you still feel that the referee's report is accurate?"

"Yes, I do," the linesman said.

I could not believe what I was hearing. It was outright lying, and the Football Association was allowing it. The evidence was plainly there, and everyone but Styles and I were patently ignoring it.

Finally, the last official from the match entered the hearing room. He also was asked to watch the film of the incident and then was asked if still stood by the head referee's report.

"No, I am sorry. I made a mistake," the third official said.

Finally, I thought, here was an honest man. Surely this will spare Styles from receiving another week's suspension.

Everyone then left the room to allow the committee to make its decision. Fifteen minutes later, we were told that Styles would be suspended for two games and given a large fine. We were also told not to discuss the meeting after leaving the Football Association.

Leaving the F.A. office, I could only think of the large percentage of players who perform each week in this great game of soccer and attempt to play by the rules and perform to the best of their ability.

After all, the game is their livelihood, and they know that if they break the rules they will pay for it. But to hold an inquiry and be judge and jury in a one-sided case filled with lies and hypocrisy seemed to me a terrible disaster for English football.

If the trials are fair, why can't the press be told?

To this day, players and coaches are fined heavily for

criticizing the decisions of referees on the field. Why is this the case?

The referees' decisions are directly impacting the livelihood of everyone involved in the game. I say let them defend their decisions in public, and the greater good will be served.

If we truly respected the game today, this would happen.

God's Helping Hand

In November of 1978, the Bell family plus 14 suitcases departed Heathrow Airport bound for six weeks in Ohio. We arrived at the airport in New York City with a plan to visit the hairdresser. My feeling was that a nice haircut, shampoo and shave would freshen me up after the long flight from London — and our three kids needed a clip too.

The layover in New York gave us limited time to relax as we waited for our next flight to Cleveland. It must have been an experience the hairdresser will never forget.

His three chairs were quickly taken up by all of us. While he worked on me, Mary would be shampooing another or using the hairdryer. You had to see it to believe it.

Entering the concourse for our flight to Ohio, we were approached by a man who asked us where we were going. He had no airline markings on his clothing, but he seemed eager to help a family of five with 14 suitcases. Gladly, we were happy to unload our cargo, never to see him again.

Boarding the plane, doubt started to enter our minds. Was he really helping us, or were we just robbed? Why did we just let him take away our luggage?

Arriving at our destination, all doubts were swept away as our baggage rolled down the ramp. Looking back on that experience in the terminal in New York, it became clear to me that the Bell family had been in the presence of an angel.

Trevor Francis: The First Million-Pound Player

During my time at Birmingham City, I had the privilege of working with Trevor Francis, both as coach and manager. Here was a young player who had been recruited by the club scout, Don Dorman, who first saw Francis in his hometown of Plymouth.

Francis was already a regular player in the first team at the age of 17. Some days, I would leave the office, stroll down the tunnel and have a chat with the groundskeeper if Francis was around.

I would just stand and watch Francis, who had come back on his own to do some additional ball work. Unknown to Francis, I would be standing in a position where he would be unable to see me watching him practice.

His time on the field was spent running with the ball from the touch line, sprinting across the field parallel with the 18-yard line and — without looking — driving the ball at goal with a ferocious shot. His technique and speed were exceptional, always firing the ball into the corner of the goal netting.

Francis became our club's top goal scorer. It practically became predictable. Whenever Francis would take the ball on the left side of the field and dribble toward the middle of the pitch about 30 to 40 yards from goal, I knew he would score.

During my second season as manager at Birmingham City, I received a call from Ron Greenwood, the England team manager. Greenwood told me he was calling Francis up for his first cap with the English national team. Greenwood asked me for advice on where Francis would best help the team on the field.

I told Greenwood that I always gave Francis a free role on the left side, playing just off the forwards on the front line.

"What do you mean by a free role?" Greenwood asked.

"I let the opponents worry about Francis," I said. "He will

score goals for you from the inside left position on the field, coming toward the center of the field as he plays the ball on his right foot."

Greenwood thanked me for my advice. I was thrilled for Francis.

When the time came for the national team match to be played, I looked forward to watching Francis don the England jersey. As I settled in front of my television to watch the game, much to my surprise Francis was lined up at right wing.

With a talented Manchester City player already lining up on the left, Greenwood apparently felt that Francis could best help his country's side by manning the right flank.

When the second half began, Francis was still lined up at right wing. But midway through the second half, I noticed a dramatic change. Francis began to move into his more familiar role, attacking from the left side, and the game began to turn.

Francis was outstanding during that half. When he was selected for his second cap with the national team, he was no longer lined up at right wing. He was back to his old familiar position on the left — the one for which he was born to play.

As team manager for Birmingham City, I received many calls offering an open checkbook for Francis. I didn't tell the board of Birmingham City, but I turned down every offer to buy Francis.

Who wants to sell the best player that Birmingham City ever had?

When I eventually left Birmingham City and Sir Alf Ramsey took over as team manager, Francis was sold for a million pounds. Ramsey lasted about six months.

As I look back over that era, the sale of Francis marked the beginning of the end for a once-great football club. To this day, Birmingham City has never fully recovered from the loss of Francis, one of the greatest English footballers of all time.

Today, Francis is a TV analyst for the Barclay's Premier League, and a good one too.

He should be — he knows the game as well as anyone I've ever coached.

One of the Most Difficult Times in Management

When a player needs to be disciplined, sometimes the consequences are kept strictly in confidence between the manager and the player, with the other players finding out only if the disciplined player tells them.

When I took over the managing job at Birmingham City, I was aware of the problems that the previous manager had with Kenny Burns.

When I arrived on the scene, Burns assured me that he would be on his best behavior and give his best effort for the club.

We had a lot of work to do, considering that we were third from the bottom of the league standings, facing a road match at Queens Park Rangers.

Burns had performed well, and I was playing him at central defender. Toward the end of the first half, we were losing the match 1-0, even though we were playing well.

Then it happened. A long ball deep into the Birmingham half was cleared by Burns after Queen Park midfielder Jonny Hollins slipped to the turf while attempting to win the ball. I watched as Burns held out his hand as though he was attempting to help Hollins to his feet.

But he wasn't offering a helping hand. Instead, he delivered a right uppercut to Hollins' jaw. Just like that, Hollins fell in a heap back to the ground. The match continued, as the officials were unaware of the incident.

With treatment, Hollins was able to continue playing in the match, and Burns thought he was "off the hook" with the referees because they had not seen the flagrant punch.

But the decision was already made in my mind. As the halftime whistle blew, I told Jim Calderwood, our substitute, to warm up while the teams came off the field. He played the entire second half in place of Burns.

We lost the match 1-0. As we left Loftus Road, the press was anxious to find out why I had benched Burns. My reply simply was that "it was an internal matter."

I hit Burns with a heavy fine. All of this was done without the press knowing the circumstances of the disciplinary action. I told Burns that if there were any more problems with him, I would make sure that everyone involved in the game would know to avoid signing him.

A year later, Burns was selected to play for the Scottish national team.

Birmingham City soon became known as a team to be reckoned with. Within three months, I sold six players and bought John Connelly and Gary Jones, both wingers, from Everton, and goalkeeper Jim Montgomery from Sunderland. They were all very talented players who helped lift the club to a new level of performance.

With the new players, Birmingham City rose to the top half of the league standings after barely escaping relegation during the previous season.

Then it happened again. We were playing at our home stadium, St. Andrews, versus Everton. I was looking forward to another victory. The Blues, as we were affectionately called by our fans, controlled most of the possession that day, but Burns just sort of strolled around, lacking any real effort.

I waited until halftime to address this with Burns in the locker room.

As I went around the dressing room speaking to individual players one by one, the team doctor called me over to tell me that Burns had threatened to break Trevor Francis' leg after the match.

"Why?" I asked.

Burns didn't want to play for Birmingham City anymore, and he thought he could convince Francis to simply "stroll around" as well. Francis, however, had too much character for that, and he refused to comply.

A few days later, I learned through a close business associate that Burns had been wrongfully approached by another club. The manager of Nottingham Forest, Brian Clough — a fellow who would later replace Revie as manager of Leeds United for a tumultuous month and a half — had told Burns that he wanted him to play for Nottingham.

Burns had been pushing me to simply release him.

A few more days later, I received a call from Peter Taylor, Clough's right-hand man. "Willie," Taylor said, "I see you are selling Kenny Burns. What's the fee?"

My reply was, "Make me an offer."

"OK," said Taylor. "I will speak to Brian and get back to you."

The very next day, I received a call with an offer to buy Burns. I told Taylor that I would take the offer to the Birmingham City board of directors and then let him know of the board's decision.

At the board meeting, Chairman Mr. Coombs was ecstatic at the offer from Nottingham Forest. "Well done, Willie," he said.

I followed his comment by saying, "I think I can get more for Burns. I will not accept the offer."

The directors were stunned. Mr. Coombs let me know that this could be costly for me. I knew what he meant. My job was on the line.

Of course, the board knew nothing of the wrongful approach of Burns. I kept this to myself, knowing that on the board we had Mr. Jack Wiseman, who was also a member of the Football Association Committee.

Wiseman would have opened up an inquiry, derailing any deals that could be made, and it would be difficult to keep my business friend — who had shared in confidence with me the news about Burns being wrongfully approached – out of the investigation.

Taylor called me again the very next day.

"Well, Willie, is the deal on?" he asked.

"No, we want more for the player," I said, as I increased the offer by another figure.

Taylor was upset, saying, "I'll have to go back to our chairman and see what he says."

The next day, Burns was a Nottingham Forest player.

Burns played well for Nottingham and became Player of the Year. This caused some of the Birmingham City supporters to question my judgment on Burns.

Then it happened yet again. Nottingham Forest was playing Arsenal in London. Burns was given a red card and sent off for misconduct. I watched the incident on television.

Arsenal had a free kick at the edge of the Forest penalty area. Burns was seen looking at the linesman and the referee, hoping they would not see him butt the Arsenal player on the back of his head, knocking the player unconscious.

But Burns was not so fortunate this time. His flagrant action was seen by the officials and he was properly disciplined.

It was not too long before Nottingham Forest got tired of Burns' act as well, and he was on the move yet again.

SEVEN

An Encounter with a Legend

*"For I am not ashamed of the gospel of Christ,
for it is the power of God unto salvation to everyone that believeth;
to the Jew first, and also to the Greek."*
— ROMANS 1:16

Following my life-changing experience in that small chapel in Ohio, I returned to England to resume my coaching career. I had just been appointed head coach and manager of Lincoln City a few months prior to our game against Watford.

Elton John, who had invested heavily in the Watford Club, entered the directors' box. He was an extremely colorful character, dressed in a black leather coat and hat and sported, as usual, outlandishly large eyeglasses. When I sat next to him, my thoughts turned to the impact that this brilliant musician could have on millions of fans if he were to experience the same life-changing love of Christ that I had only a few months before.

The game ended in a 1-0 loss for our team. The victory almost clinched a promotion for Watford to the top English league.

In the board room following the final whistle, champagne was flowing, with the imbibers either commiserating or celebrating. As I entered the room, my mind was on Elton. I had read an article in a newspaper in which the writer said that Elton would invite boys into his garden to play soccer with him.

I was well aware that some of the seemingly blessed people in our world were often among the loneliest.

I plucked up the courage to go over to Elton and ask if I could speak with him in private. He politely agreed. As we made our way to a corner of the room, he probably was thinking that I would inquire about a player or congratulate him on the result.

"Let me tell you about Jesus Christ, Elton," I said. "He is the most important person in the world for you and me." As I spoke to this precious soul, I had his undivided attention, but I did not know how to lead him to Christ. I had only been a Christ-follower for a few weeks.

"Well," I said. "Thank you for your time. I wish you and your team well."

Elton looked me directly in the eye, squeezed my arm, and said, "Thank you."

I glimpsed a tear in his eye.

Months later, I came home and sat down to watch the Parkinson Show on TV. Michael Parkinson's guest was Elton John. The music superstar had just returned from a dinner engagement and was still holding the menu. Parkinson asked Elton to sing the menu. Elton then proceeded to sing the menu in his usual brilliant fashion.

The two men then began to discuss the singer's latest album, "A Song for Guy." Elton had written the song upon the loss of his close friend in a motorcycle accident.

Parkinson asked his guest, "Now you have another possible gold record. What are your thoughts at this time?"

"My soul," Elton said, quietly. His reply floored me.

Parkinson fumbled for a response as he quickly changed the subject.

Death had become real to Elton John following the loss of his best friend. My prayer is that more dedicated Christians will care enough to try to help Elton John find the peace his soul craves in God.

Interestingly, that was not my first encounter with a legend of the British music scene. Prior to leaving Lincoln City to become a coach in America, I had received a call from the United States Soccer Federation.

They told me that the Detroit Express of the North American Soccer League was in need of a coach, and their owner wanted to meet with me about the opening. His name was Peter Frampton, lead guitarist for The Who.

Frampton owned the professional team in Michigan but lived in London. He knew about my career as a player and coach in England and thought that I would be a good fit for managing his investment in the U.S.

I flew to New York City to meet with Frampton at a Park Avenue hotel and interview for the job. He clearly wanted me, but there was a catch. He wanted me to build the franchise around a player who had developed a rather rough reputation as a bad character in the English First Division.

Frampton's plan was to bring this player to America, sign him and make him the star personality of the Detroit Express. I, on the other hand, knew this player all too well and wanted absolutely nothing to do with him. I politely declined Frampton's offer.

EIGHT

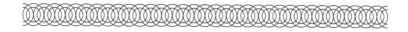

Back to School: Answering an Irishman's Call

"And we know that all things work together for good
to them that love God, to them who are the called
according to His purpose."
— ROMANS 8:28

I was coaching the Lincoln City football club in England and experiencing some success. Asked to take over the club when it was mired at the bottom of the English Third Division standings, we managed to climb halfway up the league table and safely remove the team from threat of relegation, finishing in the top half.

In British soccer, that's the ultimate humiliation: Finish in the bottom three of the league standings, and you end up being demoted to the next lower division.

Having escaped that fire, I was starting to enjoy some success in my coaching career again when I received a call from America. A group known as Athletes in Action — a Christian organization that used sports to reach young people with the gospel of Christ — called and asked if I would consider coaching a soccer team in the U.S.

When they told me that I would have to raise my own support, I literally threw their brochure into the trash. They

wanted me to leave behind a professional coaching job in
England, move myself and my young family to America, and then
basically raise my support money so that we wouldn't starve?

It didn't seem to make any sense at all — at least it didn't as
long as I rejected the notion that God might be calling me to a
new life with a higher purpose.

After reconsidering the coaching offer from AIA, I asked
Lincoln City in 1978 for two weeks of leave so that I could work
with a group of young soccer players in Tustin, California, the
main office of AIA, only to volunteer to coach for two weeks that
I would use as vacation.

When I met with the leadership of AIA, they told me that
they had been praying for God to send them a soccer coach. They
said that if I committed to coach for them, they would help me
get my green card.

It was obvious that they needed a coach badly, and Mary and
I were beginning to feel God work on our hearts. So I decided to
travel to London and meet with the head of Campus Crusade for
Christ — the parent organization of AIA. They graciously agreed
to pay my salary until I could raise my support. They also said I
could remain in the U.S.

They asked me to meet with them in Fort Collins, Colorado,
where I would meet with their soccer players and begin to coach
them. Mary and I would take Bible classes each morning and I
would coach the players each afternoon.

Another group of players learned about our team and asked
if they could play us. We agreed, not fully realizing the impact of
that decision.

When it came time to play the match, the field was packed.
Several thousand people turned out to watch us play.

Even though my team was winning 4-0 at halftime, I was
disappointed. Even though my boys were winning, they were
not playing football properly. I told them in the locker room at
halftime that their performance was a disgrace — harsh words, for
sure, but accurate ones.

We went on to win the game, 6-0. I turned to my wife Mary after the game and told her that God was leading me to work with these boys and teach them the right way to play soccer — for the Lord. Mary said, "I feel the same."

We traveled back to England to square up our affairs with the chairman of the Lincoln City football club. Our new life in America was about to begin.

This time, when I traveled across the Atlantic Ocean back to America, I was filled with a newfound sense of purpose and excitement. I had done my homework at Campus Crusade for Christ, and I had a distinct impression that God was pushing me to become a leader of young men for the cause of Christ in the U.S.

I went back to California for another meeting with AIA. This was the most exciting and energizing period of my life. My desire was to coach kids in a park and share the love of Jesus — and it helped that the sport of soccer was spreading quickly on the West Coast of America.

Kids came to the Lord when we worked with them and coached them. My players would share the message of Christ with young kids while I witnessed to the parents. We were competing against semi-pro teams and universities in Southern California, and we never lost a game. Some of the young men I coached went on to become university soccer coaches, and some became pastors of churches.

The time came when I needed to get my visa. I soon found out that I was not guaranteed a green card, and I needed to begin raising my own support. That's when I heard the fateful news from AIA in California: "We don't pay salaries," they said. "All staff must raise their own support."

Even though the head of Campus Crusade for Christ in London had promised me a salary in America until I could raise my support, there was nothing I could do. I was in dire straits. I had to support my family, but now I needed a miracle.

Charlie Sturgess, head of soccer for AIA, took me and my family to the American Embassy in Tijuana, Mexico, in an attempt to secure a visa. We were seeking the official approval we needed from the U.S. government in order to remain legally in America. Our visitor's visa had only a few days to go.

When we arrived at the embassy, it was empty. I asked Mary to take our three children, find a quiet corner, and pray.

I was only allowed to stay in the U.S. for six months with my visa, and I was about to be deported from the country. Finally, miraculously, an official came back, put our passports down and stamped them. He told us that we could stay in the U.S. for another six months. The taxi that had dropped us off at the embassy was still outside. When God moves, He moves.

Reaching the border, we all stood there, prayed and thanked the Lord for delivering us this miracle. Even the Mexican men standing around us were amazed, and they wanted to sell us statues of Mary the Mother of Jesus.

When I returned to California, I had no idea that I wouldn't be staying there for long.

Barely back in the country, I received a phone call out of the clear blue from an Irishman by the name of Ed Dobson. A soccer lover himself, Dobson said he used to watch me play. I was his hero, he said.

But he wasn't calling just to give me adulation as a fan; he wanted me to be his coach. As dean of students at Liberty Baptist College in Lynchburg, Va., Dobson served double duty by coaching the men's soccer team.

He loved soccer, and he loved coaching, but he knew he couldn't remain as coach and still fulfill all his duties as dean.

What would happen next would change my life forever.

When Ed Dobson called, I didn't know much about Liberty Baptist College. I barely knew much about America. We had only recently immigrated to the United States, and most of our brief time in the country had been in either Ohio or California.

I had spent time in Massillon, a small town on the edge of Amish country near Canton in Stark County, Ohio, and I had coached in Los Angeles — the largest metropolitan area in the nation. One extreme or the other, it seemed.

I had certainly never set foot in Virginia, much less the Blue Ridge Mountains of South Central Virginia. One trip to Lynchburg would change my life.

Dobson would be the man God would use to effect that change. Growing up as a child in Ireland, Dobson said he would often watch me play for Leeds and would dream of becoming a soccer player just like me one day. I was his childhood hero, he said.

When he found out that I had signed on to coach a bunch of young college kids for Athletes in Action in Southern California, Dobson had another idea — why not reach out and see if he could coax his childhood idol into becoming his college's coach?

So he called me while I was still coaching in California and popped the question: Would I consider taking the head coaching job at Liberty in Lynchburg, Va.?

We were doing well at AIA, so it was not a given that I would move. We agreed to travel to Virginia and visit with Dobson and the college for about three or four days.

I met Dr. Jerry Falwell there for the first time. I didn't even know who he was — even though media reports were constantly reminding every American who he was — the founder of Thomas Road Baptist Church and Liberty Baptist College, famous television evangelist and host of the Old Time Gospel Hour, and leader of the conservative Moral Majority political movement.

At the time, back in 1979, none of that meant anything to me. I was still getting used to this concept of coaching young men how to play the game the right way in my newfound home of America. More than anything, I wanted to mold these boys into men who would play for the Lord and exemplify the Spirit of Christ both on and off the field.

Stepping on campus on "Liberty Mountain" in Lynchburg came as a bit of a shock. A fledgling school of a couple of thousand students, and barely 8 years old, the college looked more like a construction zone. There was nothing but red clay and a few trailers on campus. Where were the classroom buildings? Where were the dorms? Where were all the young college students?

I told Dobson quite frankly that God would have to show me if this was the place for me and my family.

Dr. Falwell, a great big bear of a man with the handshake of a giant, invited several missionaries to come into town and speak that week at Thomas Road Baptist Church, one of the fastest-growing churches in America.

The church was meeting on a Wednesday evening at its Thomas Jefferson-style chapel on Thomas Road just a block from historic Lynchburg College. Students were bused in from the mountain and downtown to attend the service, called a Prayer Meeting.

Falwell spoke bluntly to me even as he addressed the entire congregation: "You have been listening to missionaries this week," the pastor said. "If God has been leading you, please come and pray with me."

I bowed my head in prayer. When I lifted my head, there were 70 to 80 students at the front of the worship center praying. I turned to my beloved wife, Mary, who was also praying, and said, "This is for the world."

I went back that night and told Dobson that we were coming to accept the position at Liberty. We then went back home to California and packed up for our next adventure: our cross-country move to Virginia.

Unlike the English Premier League, there were no exorbitant transfer fees to facilitate the relocation. We rented a U-Haul and packed up like the Beverly Hillbillies for the move to Lynchburg.

It was, in many ways, the beginning of the most wonderful time of my life. God pushed me out of California and on toward Liberty. God was just beginning to move on Liberty Mountain, and I was about to become a part of that movement for the next 20 years.

I informed AIA that God had called me to accept the head

coaching job at Liberty. I still had that visa stamped from Tijuana, so I had to return to the American embassy before flying back to Virginia.

Falwell found a great lawyer for me, and we went up to Washington, D.C., and I received my green card. Today, I am an American citizen. Back then, I was just another man who wanted to be.

It wasn't easy building a program at Liberty. A small, private Christian college with no soccer history, no tradition and no players of note, Liberty presented me with the ultimate coaching challenge: Build a team from scratch.

That's exactly what we did.

Dobson had done a fine job assembling a rag-tag group of players into a serviceable small college side that could compete well with other small schools. From 1975 to 1979, under Dobson, the Liberty Flames compiled a record of 38 wins, 32 losses and 2 ties.

In order to field a competitive team, I knew we would have to do better, and we would have to do better against more competitive teams. And to do that we needed players.

My first order of business was to expand Liberty's athletic horizons and look to the international game to provide a pipeline of talent. Recruiting players from all over America, as well as Mexico, England and Africa, became my calling card.

The big breakthrough for Liberty came in my third year, 1982, when we landed one of the school's best recruiting classes ever. Four of those recruits hailed from one very poor city, Accra, in Ghana, West Africa — goalkeeper Paul Annan, defender Samuel Johnson, midfielder Edward Tetteh, and forward David "Kilo" Abednego.

Playing alongside midfielder Dan Devilbiss of Mexico, forward Marshall Worthington of Lynchburg, forward Tommy Wait of Hinsdale, N.H., and defender Ron Starner of Lakeland, Fla., the quartet from Ghana formed the nucleus of what would become one of most successful teams ever at Liberty.

A 12-4 season in 1983 served as a harbinger for what was to come. Annan quickly established himself as the best goalkeeper in NCAA Division II in America, earning All-American honors for three consecutive years. His teammate and fellow countryman, Sam Johnson, earned the same accolades as our team's sweeper on the back line. With these two rocks at the back, opposing teams faced a tall order trying to find the back of our net.

From 1983 to 1986, Worthington — son of legendary Liberty baseball coach Al Worthington, scored a team-leading 30 goals, while Wait tallied 27.

The blending of this mesh of international talent led to our best season ever in the fall of 1985, when Liberty registered a record 14 wins against just 2 losses and 3 draws. Annan played the season of his life, holding opponents to just 0.35 goals per game — a mark that still stands as the best all-time in Liberty soccer history.

Liberty finished that year ranked 14th in the nation in NCAA Division II after reaching as high as No. 8 earlier in the season. Victories over national powers Alabama-Huntsville and King's College solidified our team as one of the country's best.

But that's not even what makes me the proudest. Victories that we earned off the field — and what these young men would go on to do with their lives — were the biggest rewards.

After earning a hard-fought victory over Guilford College of Guilford, N.C., on our home field in Lynchburg, I felt God leading me to share my life story with the team we had just defeated. I could tell that their coach really didn't want me to speak to his players, but God intervened and their team bus broke down.

I walked into the visitors' locker room after the game and told the Guilford team that we would fix their bus for them. While still chatting with the players, I had the opportunity to share my testimony with them.

I shared with them the most important part of my life — my

relationship with Jesus Christ. I asked them, "If you were to get in an accident in this van on your way home, do you know where you would go for eternity?"

We prayed, and the entire team raised their hands to indicate that they had accepted the Lord Jesus as their Savior. The equipment manager came up to me later and said he had been praying for that to happen to this team for two years.

Miraculously, this was not an isolated incident. Over my 21-year coaching career at Liberty, God intervened countless times to allow me to share my testimony with opposing teams. On numerous occasions, players and coaches who had been our adversaries on the pitch immediately became our brothers in Christ.

Skeptics might scoff at such sudden transformations, and that's OK. The proof comes in the form of changed lives.

Just a couple of years ago, Mary and I were having dinner at a restaurant near our home in Bluffton just outside Hilton Head, S.C., when a young man in his 40s came over to greet us at our table.

"You don't remember me," he said, "but I remember you. You were the coach of Liberty back in the 1980s when I was playing soccer for Guilford College. We played a match against you and your team in Lynchburg, Va. We lost the game that day to you and your team, but after the match you were kind enough and cared enough about us as real individuals to come witness to us and share your life story. I was one of the young men who got saved that day, and it changed my life forever."

Mary and I practically broke down in tears of joy as this young man, now a husband and father and successful business-man, shared his personal journey of faith with us.

He is just one of hundreds of changed lives that continue to thrive today because God cared enough to choose me for a task.

My final record at Liberty, the history books say, was 198 wins, 140 losses, and 40 ties.

But those aren't the real wins that I'm counting.

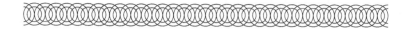

NINE

Plea from Prison: Death in a Cell

*"I am come that they might have life,
and that they might have it more abundantly."*
— JOHN 10:10

The fastest 20 years of my life happened at Liberty University. During that time, I never imagined that God was preparing me for yet another mission field.

One day everything changed in an instant.

I was resting at home playing with our collie, Chance. I was trying to give him his medicine when I felt a terrible pain in my chest. I told Mary that I was fading out, and my family called for an ambulance. My son Andrew started praying.

The ambulance came down our road and somehow managed to pass right by our house. Andrew went out into the street and screamed at them to come back. They heard his cry for help and immediately turned around.

Quick medical attention, combined with a heavy dose of God's grace, saved my life. After the hospital in Lynchburg gave me a heart catheterization, the doctor looked at me and said, "You are an accident waiting to happen."

Four of my arteries to my heart were almost completely closed. I needed quadruple bypass surgery.

Mary looked at me and said, "If you don't survive the operation, you will see the Lord."

I knew that, and that knowledge — more than anything — motivated me to go through the hospital and share my faith in God with others. One man whom I witnessed to accepted Christ as his personal Lord and Savior. Another young man listened to my words but rejected the call of the gospel.

Before my critical surgery, I prayed to the Lord and said, "If I go to see the Lord tomorrow, I don't have much to lay at His feet. If I get through this, I am totally available to serve Him anytime, anywhere."

The simple truth is, if you are totally available, you know it's for real and there is no fear.

The next day, as I awaited my heart operation, I met a young guy who was dying with internal bleeding. I decided to share my testimony with the young lad, and he accepted Jesus as his Savior.

My heart surgery was successful, and in five days the hospital released me to go home and continue my recovery. When I returned to my house in Lynchburg, I was greeted by two letters from England.

The letters came from two Christian inmates in prison there. Both appealed to Mary and me to come see them.

The letters came from HM Prison Feltham, more commonly known a Feltham Young Offenders Institution, in the London Borough of Hounslow, in southwest London.

Operated by Her Majesty's Prison Service, Feltham is widely regarded as the most violent young offenders institution in all of England. Back in 1993, conditions were at their worst.

A suicidal climate had taken over the prison, with boys killing themselves by hanging. A couple of the boys who had turned to Christ knew of my reputation as a former Scottish soccer player who had left England to coach at a Christian college in America. So they reached out to me and my wife, in hope that we would come back to speak to their fellow prisoners.

Our hearts were broken for them, and we knew that this is why God had spared me. He was calling us to go back to England — not to coach — but to bring the love of Christ to the most desperate souls in a troubled land.

When we arrived at Feltham, we began to ask questions about the hangings.

As we probed into the circumstances of the many deaths, it became clear to us that a climate of occult practices had infiltrated the prison. Many of the boys were making Ouija boards and playing Satanic games on them.

We were allowed to tell the boys about the Lord. They immediately got rid of the boards and the hangings stopped. We were allowed to stay all day every day for six weeks. By the time we left, the boys were attending two church services a day.

Michael Brundle was the chaplain at Feltham at the time. He was very happy to work with us. We were like a mom and dad to these boys. Mary would frequently tell the young lads that she loved them.

When the suicides stopped, we felt that it was safe to leave the prison and take our ministry to inmates in other institutions around England. That's when we founded Within the Walls, our newfound calling and full-time ministry.

Our mission was summed up by John 17:3: "And this is eternal life, that they might know the only true God, and Jesus Christ whom thou has sent."

An adult inmate in HM Highpoint Prison in Stradishall told us, "If someone had only shared the Lord with me as a young offender, I might not be in prison today."

While British prisons are largely secular in nature and often reluctant to allow ministers of the gospel on the premises, my standing as a respected soccer player and coach in England gave me access that others could not enjoy. While the young offenders were confined to a life behind bars for many years, God opened those prison cells to me and let me in.

Within the Walls is focused on taking the good news of Jesus Christ to the inmates who desperately need a message of hope and forgiveness, regardless of their crimes.

During our many visits, we would conduct discussion groups,

hold musical concerts, and stand ready with Bible materials for all who showed interest. Through the ministry of Within the Walls, many prisoners have come to know the Lord and have gone on to grow in their newfound faith.

We even received the endorsement of the Governor and Chaplaincy of Her Majesty's Prison Service:

"Bill and Mary came in as two ordinary people to speak to a bunch of pathetic, difficult people," said Joe Whitty, who at the time was Governor of Feltham Prison. "Within the Walls has been totally accepted by the staff owing to your spontaneity. It has affected the behavior of many boys. The main thing that happened was that youngsters for the first time have looked within themselves in a way that may change their lives. Boys are now speaking to staff about their faith. We have been able to reinforce that. This is missing in most prisons. The staff has become more caring. You've brought a soul to this place."

The chaplain, Rev. Michael Brundle, said that "Bill and Mary brought love, real love. You cannot package that, and the lads respond to it. I have been ministered to by Within the Walls after 12 years as a minister. Can we have them back tomorrow?"

And Carol Smith Stanley, one of our counselors and board members, said, "Within the Walls is an exciting ministry that brings the gospel to young people in prison who desperately need a message of hope."

By the time we concluded our first period of ministry at Feltham, word about our ministry was starting to spread to other correctional facilities in England. Aylesbury Prison in Buckinghamshire was one such institution.

A place where hardened criminals were sentenced to life in prison, Aylesbury invited Mary and me to come speak to the most hardened of British offenders. Allen Marley was the chaplain at the time, and he welcomed us with open arms.

We quickly learned the two most used places in an English prison were the gym and the chaplain's office. The inmates got their frustrations out in the gym and got their heart rights with the chaplain.

Often, I would coach soccer and teach some courses on the game during my time of ministering to the inmates. We would also speak with the officers in the prisons, and many of them came to know Christ as Savior.

One day, I was invited to speak at the chapel service at the prison in Leicester. The chaplain's wife and baby had just been killed about one week earlier in a tragic traffic accident.

After I delivered the message that night, an officer in the back of the room shouted, "Dear Lord, I am a sinner!"

When the service was over, I met with this man. He came over to Mary and me and said, "When I saw how the chaplain responded to this horrific tragedy in his life — when I saw how he relied totally on his faith and trust in the Lord — that is what saved me. I wanted what he had. I wanted that same sense of peace and complete trust in God."

People are watching us. When people say that they are Christians, they better walk the talk. That officer at the prison in Leicester is now saved for eternity because of the testimony of that one chaplain. That is a true story. That is why the way we live our lives is so important.

What we found throughout the prisons in England is that the men behind bars were looking for forgiveness and love — the two things that were missing the most in their lives.

The young offenders were so desperate for anyone to love them that they would often line up for a hug from Mary.

God has continued to perform miraculous works inside the British prison system. At Aylesbury, I brought a trunkload of posters of American football players to pass out to the inmates. One inmate, whose nickname was Spider, offered to help me pass them out.

The inmates were so desperate to receive posters of American football players, and this one helpful inmate was no exception. He was just happy to be part of something bigger than himself.

For the most part, these men will leave prison with the same clothes there were wearing when they were first incarcerated. One day, I saw a young man waiting for the bus as he was preparing to leave the prison yard. I offered him my watch, and I had to force him to take it.

Most of these inmates are not experiencing the love of Christ. One boy's mother actually wrote him a letter that stated, "When are you going to get out and start stealing again and caring for me?"

The reality is that we are all in prison when we are without Christ. I know that this was true of me when I was addicted to the sport of soccer. Sports can take over your life and become your prison.

In my case, God chose to rescue me from this prison and replace it with a love for Christ and a passion to help others. Now, I only want to pass it on.

Women's Prison: An Answer to Prayer

I was arriving in Delaware to meet a brother in the Lord for lunch. He had founded a prison ministry there many years before. It was an opportunity to seek advice about such a ministry as our vision for Within the Walls had just been given to Mary and me from the Lord.

The lunch went very well. Our conversation was focused on the prison system and the open door that God had given to us to take the Gospel to incarcerated souls.

My friend Bill asked me, "Bill, would you speak tonight at a women's prison? Please take my place. I have, as part of my ministry, a weekly Wednesday night service for women inmates."

"Of course," I said. "It is always a privilege to tell people about Jesus."

That evening, the women filed into the chapel and took up the front four rows. As I looked across their faces, I saw women who were old enough to be my mother and others younger than my daughter. All were smiling, glad to be away from the cells.

Some were literally glowing with the joy of the Lord.

My friend announced: "I would like to introduce Coach Bill Bell from Liberty University."

As I approached the podium, a young girl began to weep openly and continued to do so through the entire message. Perhaps she had received bad news that day, or maybe she was just depressed, I thought.

Twenty minutes later, as the women lined up to shake my hand, the young girl approached me.

"Are you OK? Is anything bothering you," I asked.

"No," she said. "I am so happy. God has just answered my prayer tonight."

She then proceeded to tell me that she had been praying all day for God to show her that He still cared for her. "Give me a sign, something that will assure me that you are still there," she prayed.

She also told me that she had two children. "Tonight, when I heard that you were from Liberty University and lived in Lynchburg, Va., I could not contain my joy. You see, I have graduated from Liberty and I am from Lynchburg. God is so good! Tonight He showed me that He still cares for me."

Leaving Delaware, I took with me many good ideas about prison ministry, but the most lasting impact came from a woman who had encouraged me beyond words.

A Man Named Bob

Approaching Long Lartin, I see walls that could not be climbed due to the large tube-like contraptions lining the prison's perimeter. Lights were everywhere.

Entering the prison, I pass through many gates, the cameras watching my every move. Men with dogs walk around the grounds inside the fence. It was here that I came to coach the inmates.

Some of the young men behind bars were members of the Irish Republican Army. Some of them had committed crimes so heinous that they were confined to Long Lartin for a very long time.

The soccer session went well. Within a half hour, the game of soccer had bridged the gap between us. All of the inmates responded to me.

Later that day, I had grew to enjoy the men's company. Their work rate and interest in my coaching session were great, and the results showed in more ways than one.

Later that evening, we met in a classroom where I would speak on the game and then tell them about my faith in the Lord. Again, it was a great time. Their questions were general, but I felt that they just enjoyed the refreshing change of meeting an athlete and coach.

With about 30 minutes left, my thoughts and speaking focused on their salvation. "You know, lads," I said, "we are all sinners. And I want to tell you about someone who can take all your sins away."

Suddenly, from across the room came a broad Scottish accent, shouting, "I am not a sinner! I didn't kill the old woman!"

This man then proceeded to stand up and point to an inmate sitting in the corner. "He's the sinner! He sins!"

A short silence shadowed the room as I looked at the accused man.

"Hold it right there," came a voice from the back of the room. A man who looked like John the Baptist, because of his long beard hanging down to his chest, interrupted the silence.

In for armed robbery, this man went on to tell the Scotsman that he deserved to be in prison. "Listen to Willie," he said.

The Scotsman left the room saying, "I appreciate what you're saying, Bob, but I'm leaving."

The rest of the evening went very well, as a number of the inmates made decisions for Christ. As they left the room, a young man came up to me and shook my hand.

He told me that just a few days before my visit, he had

accepted Christ as his Lord and Savior.

"Praise the Lord," I said. "What happened?"

"Big Bob led me to the Lord," he replied.

Leaving Long Lartin, I felt like I had just left Paul the Apostle — a man who had given his life to see others come to the saving knowledge of Jesus Christ.

Bob Campbell, a servant of God — still in prison at Her Majesty's Prison, the Verne in Portland, but still sharing his Savior. Still making a stand.

Lewes Prison: God's Timing

It was a beautiful English morning as I drove to the Lewes Prison in the county of Sussex. That morning the chapel was full, with half the crowd wearing the establishment's denim uniform, and the other half still in their street clothes while they waited to appear in court.

The service went well as the Lord helped me convey His love and purpose for the lives of these troubled men. Many positive decisions were made that day, and men's lives were changed forever.

Two years later, I was back in England to visit the other end of the country. Again, I used soccer as a platform to tell the men about Jesus. The response was tremendous and the Lord was glorified.

After the service, a young inmate approached me with a joyful grin. "Do you remember me, Willie?"

"I am not sure. Where did we meet?"

He proceeded to tell me that he was in remand at Lewes Prison awaiting his sentence two years earlier when I came to speak there. "You said exactly the same things today, but today I have accepted Jesus Christ as my Savior."

Leaving there, I remembered the Lord's words: "Some plant, some water. But God gives the increase."

A Lesson Learned: A Boy Named Peter

This was to be another fruitful visit to Feltham Prison. It was 1995.

God had allowed Mary and me the privilege of seeing many young men turn their lives around at this place.

One young man named Peter called and asked Mary and me if we would visit him regularly. This we did, with great joy, as Peter indicated to us that he was a Christian and that Jesus meant more to him than anyone or anything else.

It did not take us long to know that Peter was a very intelligent young man. In fact, he was capable of achieving success at a university.

Mary and I discussed at length about possibly asking Liberty University Chancellor Dr. Jerry Falwell if the young man could be given a scholarship to attend Liberty. We eventually put the thought to Peter, and he was overjoyed. With his sentence almost complete, America would be a dream come true.

Later that year, with Falwell's blessing, Peter was invited to join the student body at Liberty, with all of his expenses paid for by the school.

Unfortunately, his time at Liberty was short-lived. Within two weeks, he was before the deans after breaking the campus rulebook. In fact, he was fortunate that the local police were not informed of the incident.

Our disappointment showed. The thoughts of a young offender turning his life around at Liberty University were gone. But we did not give up hope for Peter. We called our good friend Ed Dobson. The man who had brought us to Liberty was now the pastor of a large church in Grand Rapids, Michigan.

Dobson felt that if Peter were willing, Dobson's church in Grand Rapids would pay for the boy to attend college at Word of Life Bible Institute in Upstate New York. There would be much more discipline there than there was at Liberty, and it would represent another chance for Peter.

The young man accepted this generous offer through tears

of joy. Two months went by with good reports of Peter's conduct coming from Word of Life.

Then the same trait came back, as Peter committed a similar offense. This time there would be no second chance. He was expelled from the school.

A few weeks later, we received another call from Peter. "I have been accepted into St. Johns University," he said. "They will give me a scholarship to play soccer."

We still receive occasional calls from Peter. His conversation is mainly about soccer now. Somehow, his relationship with the Lord has diminished.

Mary and I have prayed that Peter achieves his bachelor's degree, but more importantly, that he again trusts totally in Jesus Christ, the One who took him from a life in prison in England to a state university in the U.S. We pray that someday Peter recognizes this and gives all the glory to God.

Perhaps a very important lesson will one day be learned by Peter.

It was certainly a lesson learned by Mary and me.

Shaftsbury: The Love of Christ

Here we were, Mary and I, visiting a youth correctional center on the outskirts of the picturesque town of Shaftsbury, for a Christmas service.

All went well. The center's church was full with not only young men but also visitors from the local churches.

Later that evening, everyone was ushered into a large hall for tea and Christmas cake. This gave Mary and me time to speak to the boys and hopefully convey God's love before we had to leave.

While I was speaking to two of the inmates, I noticed that Mary was over at the other side of the room speaking to another young boy named Patrick.

As they were leaving to go back to their cells, I saw a group of young men lining up to hug Mary before leaving.

Patrick had asked Mary: "How can Jesus love me after all the wrong I have done?"

Mary's reply was given with the Lord's compassion. She told Patrick that Jesus Christ loved him so much that He died on the cross. She also told him that Mary loved him, and it was Jesus in Mary that loved him.

At that point, Patrick threw his arms around Mary and told her that no one had ever told him that they loved him. This was the start of a long line of young men wanting to hear that someone loved them.

That evening, the prison warden's wife came to know the Lord Jesus Christ as her Savior. We also prayed that Patrick and the other young men would receive this same wonderful gift of eternal life.

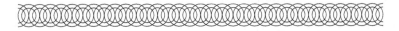

Poems by the Inmates

You Will Catch My Tears
When my thoughts deny my body sleep
When despair overtakes me and my fears go deep
I worry not because I know
You will catch my tears.

When the light goes out and the darkness wins
When the silence of night recreates my sins
I worry not because I know
You will catch my tears.

In you, Lord, I am free in soul if not in body
I know, Lord, that you will be with me through the years
And always be there to catch my tears.
— *British Youth Offender, February 1994*

Rest
Rest will often come to us at evening, when we pray
However simple are the words that we have knelt to say

And if we take a well-known book, and turn its pages through
How often can we lose ourselves, for just an hour or two
Rest may come with someone dear, a friendly little chat
A joke, a laugh, a new idea, talk of this and that
Or walking through the woods at dawn
To hear the blackbirds sing
Brings music to our tired hearts, and gentle comforting
So rest, dear friend, when life becomes
Almost too much to bear
Find comfort in the simple joys that meet us everywhere
The robin with its bright red breast, the lark in skies of blue
In all these small but lovely things
Rest comes to me and you.

John, an orderly for the chaplain in Wealston, Yorkshire

HOW LONG HAVE YOU BEEN CHASING DREAMS?

How long have you been chasing dreams
And organizing various schemes?
The castle you would build, would be so high
You're not the only one, you know
Who started with, Get up and go
Only to see them fade away and die

Are you the kind that tried again
But found the sunshine turn to rain
And all your greatest efforts turn to dust?
Then you can have smile on me
I've shared in such calamity
The best of my ideas all went bust

There is, despite this awful mess
An answer to your pain and stress
A way out of this bitter veil of tears
You'll find that Jesus is the way
And that it's Him who rules, OK?
He'll wash away your sin and all your fears

Lay all your problems at His feet

And right there, at the mercy seat
Ask Him to come and live within your heart
I know, with joy, you will acclaim
That you will never be the same
New creation, new relation and new start.

Bob Campbell, inmate

Too Late

Too late, the keeper shouted,
Closing the mighty gate.
You've had a thousand yesterdays.
Today is just too late.
You've heard so many witness
And read it with your eyes,
But you chose what the world can give,
Rejecting truth — for lies.

Too late, the keeper shouted,
Behind the inner door
Which closed off all communion
With God — for evermore.
You knew that Jesus loved you.
You heard his every call.
You saw that for this evil world,
The writings on the wall.

Too late, the keeper shouted.
Is this what you will hear?
Because the bridegroom tarried,
You believed he'd not appear.
Eternity of sadness
Could hear your every groan
About the day, you gave away
A place in heaven — home.

Bob Campbell, inmate

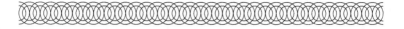

Within the Walls Ministry

Board of Directors:
Lynchburg, VA

Carol Godwin, Chairperson

Bill & Mary Bell

Charles Burks

Don Leslie

Joan Phelps

Katherine Smith

Denny Brown

Rev. David Etheridge

Barbara Irby

John Peniche

Joe Sanzone

Mary Thomas

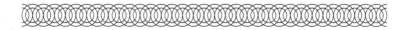

TEN

Fixing the Game:
On the Field and Off

"I have fought the good fight, I have finished the race,
I have kept the faith."
— II TIMOTHY 4:7

One of my most treasured possessions is the following letter that I received from former Liberty University Director of Athletics Kim Graham. It was upon the occasion of my retirement as head soccer coach after guiding the school's men's soccer program for 21 years.

It was dated May 7, 2001:

Dear Coach Bell:

I have admired and respected you throughout your career. Even during my time as football coach I came to know and understand that you were a man of integrity, always willing to do the right thing. As I grew to know you in my role as an athletic administrator, those traits became even more noticeable.

I will never forget your conviction against Sunday play when you decided not to coach your team in the Big South Conference championship match. That showed me you were more concerned with standing up for what you believed than with winning. Not enough men have the fortitude to do that.

The foundation you laid for the Liberty soccer program will never be forgotten. The lives that you influenced and the principles you based your decisions on will be here forever.

Thank you for giving so much of yourself to Liberty University.

Sincerely,
Kim Graham,
Director of Athletics

As someone who has devoted most of his life to either playing or coaching a sport, I truly appreciate those words from my good friend Kim Graham. His words reinforce the most important lesson that I ever learned during my two decades on Liberty Mountain: The greatest victories are those that are won off the field.

The late Dr. Jerry Falwell always used to talk about training up "young champions for Christ" whenever he spoke at Thomas Road Baptist Church or in chapel services at Liberty. His number one goal, throughout everything he endeavored to build at Liberty, was to raise up a generation of leaders of integrity.

That absolutely cannot happen without faculty, staff and coaches who commit themselves to living lives of integrity.

For Kim Graham to point out the example of my conviction — one based upon principles that supersede winning or losing — is a reward in itself, because it means that our decisions have consequences that extend beyond our lifetimes.

Every time I coached a practice or a match at Liberty, that was my goal — to influence young lives so that the boys watching and listening to me would one day truly appreciate the meaning of Christ-centered character.

Working hard in practice and giving maximum effort in each match served the higher purpose while providing more temporal rewards. But the greatest reward any of us can ever hope to hear one day are these words, "Well done, thou good and faithful servant."

Part of being a good and faithful servant is pointing out where men have sometimes gone astray. Too many times in my career, I witnessed actions and words on the field that brought shame to our sport and harm to young lives.

The win-at-all-costs mentality that pervades our game today at its highest level is the greatest shame of all. Professional football clubs will spend tens of millions of dollars to acquire players who care about no one but themselves. Referees, some of them, will accept bribes in exchange for influencing outcomes.

Club managers and owners will treat players like livestock to be bought, sold or traded at the drop of a hat. If it leads to a championship, the thinking goes, what does it matter if the life of one person is ruined?

It is this thinking that causes some players to lose their minds in the heat of battle and commit unsportsmanlike fouls on the field of play. Worse, some resort to cheating and debasing their opponents, as though winning by fraudulent means counts for anything at all.

The shame of the Lancaster Gate scandal of 1998 continues to hang over the English Football Association like a modern-day Black Plague. Bribes, power grabs, and outright cheating continue to defile our sport, even as millions line up to watch matches live or on television.

Liverpool striker Luis Suarez bites an opponent during a match and is given only a 10-game suspension. We learn that up to 600 matches worldwide may have been fixed, and where is the moral outrage?

Perhaps we shouldn't be surprised after all. After building an empire where winning is all that matters, why should we look away when players, referees and club administrators openly cheat?

Why should we blush when a player fakes an injury in an attempt to have his opponent sent off the field with a warrantless red card?

The lack of integrity is the single greatest threat to our game today, but more importantly, it threatens the very fabric of our society.

The 17-plus years that Mary and I spent ministering to young offenders behind bars in England taught us a lot of lessons, but the chief of them was this: If you compromise your principles to get ahead in life, you will do almost anything.

Without a moral compass, young men and women will commit the most heinous of crimes. They will kill, plunder, rape, steal, maim, even sell their soul.

The Savior of souls is the Lord Jesus Christ, and I will never be ashamed of the power of that truth. The good news of the Gospel radically changed my life one night in Massillon, Ohio, and it continues to change me today.

Mary and I saw firsthand the power of the Gospel to change the lives of young men and women in the hardest of Britain's prisons.

And make no mistake — when the Gospel takes hold, the change is permanent. Twenty years after I shared my testimony to the young players of Guilford College, one of those players came up to me in a restaurant in South Carolina and thanked me for sharing my faith.

It had changed his life forever, he said, and he was most grateful.

God was gracious enough to show me His light at the end of my tunnel, and my life's passion now is to share that light with everyone I meet.

That mission takes many forms — coaching and guiding young players, ministering to prison inmates and giving them love and hope, sharing words of encouragement with the sick and dying, and passing along lessons that can change the habits of today's players, officials and managers.

Before my quest here on earth is done, and before I am called home to meet my Maker, I want to share with you the reader the ten most important lessons of my life:

1) *There is nothing more important in this life than faith and trust in God.* When you are on your deathbed and looking back at the life you have lived, will you regret it, or will you welcome and embrace your entrance into eternity with open arms? Only faith and trust in Jesus Christ as your Lord and Savior will make that happen.

2) *A life lived for self is empty.* I made the mistake of living that way for most of the first 40 years of my life. Soccer was my god, and all I had to show for it — despite sustained success at the sport's highest levels — was an aching hole in my heart that could not be satisfied. It was only when I started living for others that I was made whole.

3) *The best gift you can ever give someone else is love.* Mary and I learned this lesson repeatedly every time an inmate would come up to us and call us "Mum and Dad."

4) *If you have the ability to help another person, it is your responsibility to do so.* I will never forget the look on the drowning man's face in Amsterdam as my teammates and I stood on the shore and watched the dying man float down stream.

5) *Your integrity is your greatest asset.* Never forget that your every action is being watched, and you are always leaving legacy, whether for good or bad. After you die, only your reputation survives here on this earth.

6) *Serve a higher calling.* Don't just live for today or for yourself. Live so that what you do matters in eternity. Make a difference. Change the world.

7) *Forgive the faults and shortcomings of others.* Look past offenses. Don't dwell on hurts. Thank God for using those events to build character in your life.

8) *Trust God to provide for your needs.* There were many times at Liberty when we did not know when we would see our next paycheck. Financial difficulty was the norm for a long period at Liberty, but we never went hungry. God met our every need, every single time.

9) *Pass it on.* Don't keep knowledge and wisdom to yourself. Share your life lessons with those around you, especially the young, the hurting and the hardened. They need it most.

10) *Always be thankful.* No matter what comes your way, always remember that God intended it for your good, so praise

Him for it. I truly would not change a single detail of my life. If He willed it, I accept it.

In closing, here is a poem I wrote in 2007. I call it "A Special Gift."

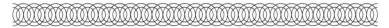

A Special Gift
They called Him Savior, Lord and Friend.
A time they thought would never end.
Then as they shared a meal with Him,
The dreaded chapter did begin.
He took the bread and blessed it as many times before.
Breaking it, His body, He did speak of
the key to Heaven's door.
He took the wine and gave it, the blood He had to spill.
These loving gifts He has given to us; they are with us still.
We can all partake of this sacred meal which on the altar lay,
Awaiting souls who love Him, to eat, drink and pray.
Come worship Him!

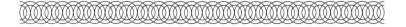

More Thoughts on the Game:
Reviewing the Past to Succeed in the Future

In 1966, Great Britain hosted the most prestigious competition in the soccer world: the World Cup.

All eyes were on Brazil, West Germany, Holland and, of course, the host country, England. Everyone knew that England had an abundance of wingers. Most professional clubs played with at least one, so talent on the flanks was plentiful.

It did not take a soccer genius to recognize that England's Alf Ramsey had decided to play the 4-3-3 system (four defenders, three midfielders and three forwards) and abandon the orthodox wide men, allowing players to interchange across the front line.

This was unknown in European circles. Ramsey had crafted

this master plan and began to confuse all who played against England.

We all know the outcome of this strategy. England became World Cup Champions and Alf Ramsey became Sir Alf Ramsey.

All of Britain hailed the achievement, and rightfully so. But the sport of soccer did not become better for it. In fact, the exact opposite happened. Schools, youth teams, amateur clubs and pro teams began to adopt the 4-3-3 tactical system of alignment.

Everyone wanted to be like the world champions. And just like that, the orthodox winger was on his way out of the game.

But it was also around this time — from the late 1960s to the early 1970s — that many good things began to take shape: more of an emphasis on third-man running, crossovers and, most important of all, the attacking fullback.

All around Europe, clubs began to employ the overlapping defender in the attack. My own club, Leeds United, adopted this strategy, which suddenly turned me into one of our team's goal scorers.

Still, this was not enough to counteract the overall defensive posturing that would quickly overwhelm the sport. The game itself became less entertaining as teams reverted into a largely defensive shell.

When the next World Cup competition came around four years later, England and the rest of the world knew the 4-3-3 system extremely well. Unfortunately, England was not so well prepared to defend against wingers ready to take them on. Having not seen much of this attacking style at the club level, British national team defenders were clueless how to stop the wide attacking players.

Perhaps the United States can learn from this. The coaches all over the U.S. are striving to be the best at their level. My advice to them is to look at your players, their talents and their individual flairs. Use them and allow them to apply their God-given talents in the natural flow of the game. Yes, look at the best in the world, but do not copy them.

Today, if you are a talented winger in Britain, you are worth your weight in gold. We just need a lot more of them.

Officials: Food for Thought

Boys everywhere dream of playing professional sports. It is only a dream until one day you find yourself rubbing shoulders with other athletes who are living out their own boyhood ambitions.

Against this backdrop, the officials do their best to police the sport. But still, I have to wonder — are we really training and equipping the best officials?

My experience in playing and coaching professionally for 22 years is that full-time officials are an absolute must for top-level soccer. Think about it. Here we have a game with 22 athletes who have been working extremely hard every day to be among the best in the world at their craft. They are physically and mentally prepared for their job. On a Saturday, they run out onto the field and place themselves under the authority of an official who has perhaps spent the week selling insurance, teaching or running a shop.

What is this official's preparation for the game? Jogging around the local public park? Working out at the local YMCA? We can do better.

Every year, the game changes. Tactics, fitness and rules are constantly renewed. This places extra demands on players and coaches. Even working diligently week in and week out does not guarantee success.

What's needed is the application of this same discipline in training and preparation for the officials. Let them train with professional team trainers; let them work five-versus-five games during the week; immerse them in the sport — and then they will be better prepared for the rigors of Saturday.

I am impressed by the way that American football players respect the decisions of their full-time officials. This is not so in soccer. It is quite sad that this lack of respect has been tolerated for so long. It is past time to change that.

It would also greatly help the sport if we could bring in those who have played the game at a very high level and train them to become officials. Why not encourage those who were among the very best in their sport to become those who police it?

Transfer Fees and Salaries: Where Will It End?

L ook at the English Premier League today. Some of the transfer fees we now see could have purchased an entire club just 10 or 15 years ago. What has happened?

Today, transfer fees are typically in the millions of pounds, and so are the average salaries of players in the EPL.

For the health and well-being of the game, it is time to consider a transfer cap and a salary cap for players. Though the players would surely protest, such caps are needed if the game is going to survive. It is also needed to create a level playing field.

The current system of exorbitant fees and wages all but ensures that the top clubs in the EPL — Manchester United, Manchester City, Chelsea, Liverpool and Arsenal — will always be the top clubs in the league. Yes, an Everton, Aston Villa or Tottenham may make an occasional run, but that is all it will be — occasional.

It is time to restore financial order in the sport, before it is too late. My fear is that if we do not implement some form of cap, several of the middle-tier to bottom-rung clubs will suffer financial collapse and fold. And players certainly do not want that to happen. Nor do the fans.

The Future of the British Game

I would be overjoyed if England were to ever repeat its success of 1966 and actually win a World Cup.

Well, over the past few years, as more international players have entered the English Premier League, England's chances of winning the world crown have diminished. Wayne Rooney is a top-class striker in the Premier League, and most everyone on the

English National Team is a world-class player as well. But without international talent around them, they go from great to merely good. The imported players enable those around them to excel.

The situation is much the same with Major League Baseball in the USA. Take away the Cuban, Mexican, Venezuelan and Dominican players, and many of the teams would not be nearly as talented as they are right now.

Which leads me to sharing my opinion on the future of American soccer. I believe that one day the American men will be far ahead of England due to the fact that women's soccer in the USA is the best in the world. Most universities in America have good soccer programs that are developing players for the national team, Major League Soccer and the women's professional league. One day, these female soccer players will be mothers with sons and daughters that will propel their respective leagues on to world status.

I am sure that the England team manager is aware of that. He is just a bit more fortunate right now to have access to a better selection of players in the Premier League — yet it is a selection of British soccer talent that is deteriorating year after year due to the influx of foreign talent.

Without increased financial support for the development of more young British players, we may never again see mighty England hoist the World Cup trophy above their heads.

* * * * * * *

Finally, if you watched the 2014 World Cup along with me, then no doubt you were as disappointed as I was to see Uruguayan and Liverpool striker Luis Suarez bite the shoulder of Italian player Giorgio Chiellini during the Uruguay-Italy match on June 24.

While Suarez was suspended for the reminder of the World Cup and four month overall by the FIFA, he should have been banned for life. This was his third incident of biting an opponent on the field of play, and this behavior is inexcusable.

In short, he should never wear the Liverpool jersey ever again.

Stand Up and Be Counted

Today, I read about the July 2013 gang fights and disciplinary problems at Feltham Prison in England. How sad to see a place that houses young men become a place where the devil takes a foothold.

Mary and I were saddened to see the place where our prison ministry began so many years ago now once again controlled by the will of Satan. During our first time of ministry there, God blessed abundantly.

The records show that the establishment became known as a place where the Lord Jesus was elevated and young men's lives were changed. Since then, the Christian influence behind these walls has waned.

First of all, let me say that I have the highest respect for the officials and officers who preside at these institutions. I know how hard they work. So the problems do not lie at the desk of the Prison Governor or his or her staffs. They are, rather, spiritual problems.

We have witnessed God moving in the lives of the inmates, and it is time for another revival within the walls.

That begins with earning the trust and the love of the young men who are behind bars. They must first know that someone loves them and wants to help them.

During our first visit to Feltham, these were the questions the young men would typically pose to Mary and me:

"Do you work for the prison?"

"No."

"Who pays you?"

"We are volunteers."

"Are you two married to each other?"

"Yes."

"Why did you come in here?"

"Because," I said, "if my brother, son or father were locked up, I would go and visit them, and we want you to know that we love you and it is God in us who loves you."

Most prisoners will ask you questions like this. They ask these questions because they want to be able to trust you. That is why they wanted to know if we were employed by the prison system. They don't trust "the system," as they refer to it, but they found it much easier to trust a couple of volunteers.

I can say now that not all visitors can be part of God's master plan. It is critical that the chaplain knows Jesus Christ as personal Savior and not be ashamed of the Gospel of Jesus. It is the good news of salvation for all, especially the young men whose lives seem lost and full of despair.

A chaplain who is a minister of God will have the discernment to know whether visitors who want to reach out to the inmates have the genuine love of God in their hearts.

I would challenge the British government as they ponder the Feltham Prison situation to get involved and do something about it. What about those sitting in Parliament who profess Christ as Savior? It is time for them to stand up and speak up. Defend the faith.

The discussion should be, "How can we introduce Jesus Christ to a lost inmate?"

After all, Christ said, "Without me, you can do nothing."

This will take more than lip service, however. It will take financial support and a commitment to send Christ-honoring men and women into the prisons.

It is nothing less than an investment for eternity.

A Final Word of Thanks

Thank you for reading this book. Perhaps some of the things mentioned have happened to you. Perhaps you are not sure if the Gospel is the power of God unto salvation.

Just remember that God's Word is so simple and truthful.

Jesus died for our sins so that we could be made right with God. All we have to do is trust Jesus to save us, forgive us of our sins, and reconcile us with God.

When I was a new Christian, I thought, why did someone not share the truth of the Gospel with me earlier?

The fact is that no other religious leader in the history of the world – other than Jesus – has ever risen from the grave.

I also want to thank the Lord for his unfailing love. I thank the Lord Jesus Christ for dying on the cross and saving me.

I pray that the Holy Spirit will touch the heart of every reader of this book.

My prayer for you is that, like me, you will find your light at the end of the tunnel — the shining light of the glory of God in Heaven.

Mary: A Special Friend, Wonderful Wife and Mother

This book — this story of my life — would not be complete without a story about the most special person in my life: Mary Bell, my wonderful wife and very special friend, and loving mother to our children.

It takes a lot to put up with a professional athlete and coach. The ups, downs, injuries, losses and all of the pressures are constantly there. Yet I can honestly say that without Mary by my side, I never would have made it at the level I did.

Her encouragement, willingness to uproot homes and follow me to where I wanted to play and coach, and her ability to raise up a family of wonderful children and keep them sheltered from the casualties of the game of soccer — all of these were essential traits.

After we had courted for about 18 months, while I was completing my engineering apprenticeship and playing amateur soccer, I was offered a nice sum of money to sign a contract with a semi-professional team. This was my chance to earn enough money to buy an engagement ring for Mary.

But when I mentioned this opportunity to her, the reply was, "I know you love me, and there is no need to give up your amateur status and be tied to playing for one club. Just enjoy your game. I know that one day we will be married."

Yes, we did get married six months later, and I continued to play amateur soccer for one more year. During that time, I was selected for the Scottish Amateur National Team.

Later, I joined Leeds United as a professional and went on to play or coach for 22 years in the English leagues.

God certainly had Mary in mind for me. Thank you, Lord, for your wonderful love in both of our lives and for letting us share the gift of your great love with each other.

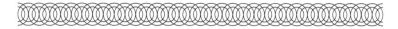

LIFE'S PATH

Expectations rise as men and women say, "We can."
All hungry to achieve ambitions and dreams,
Oblivious of the enemy they forge on, focused.

What is happening? The mirror has cracked.
The vision before them, deformed and hazy,
Uncertainty attempts to change the tempo.

It has been a growing experience,
As minds and hearts prepare for the prize
Set before them by God, for His glory
And in His time.

— *William Bell,* 1997

"Commit to the Lord whatever you do
and your plans will succeed."
PROVERBS 16:3

Final Thoughts

During the times Mary and I visit the prisons, one of the questions we ask the inmates is — "Do you believe in Jesus Christ?"

The majority will say no. A few will be honest and say yes, even with the intense peer pressure bearing down on them inside the prison.

My next question normally is — "Do you believe there is a Devil?"

Almost 100 percent of the inmates will say yes.

"Why do you believe that?" I ask.

The same reply would always come back: "Look at all the bad things that are happening in the world."

"You are right," I would respond. Jesus tells us many times in His Word about the Devil. This is the same Satan who is attempting to capture the souls of these men and women who are incarcerated for their crimes on earth.

It is sad to admit it, but too often he is winning this battle today. We need to pray for the prison chaplains as they face a spiritual battle every single day.

The only hope for the inmates is for them to be changed forever on the inside by the indwelling power and love of Jesus Christ.

For them, the only answer is Jesus.

"For God so loved the world that He gave his only begotten Son, Jesus Christ, that whosoever believes on Him should not perish but have everlasting life."
– JOHN 3:16

CPSIA information can be obtained at www.ICGtesting.com
Printed in the USA
BVOW08*0456270816

460327BV00003B/13/P